Village Gossip

Village Gossip

Joanna Capjon

assisted by

Lucinda Green, MBE

PELHAM BOOKS
London

First published in Great Britain by
Pelham Books Ltd
27 Wrights Lane
London W8 5TZ
1987

British Library Cataloguing in Publication Data

Capjon, Joanna
    Village Gossip.
    1. Village Gossip (Horse)
    I. Title
    798.2′4   SF295.187.V5

ISBN 0–7207–1744–2

Typeset by Cambrian Typesetters, Frimley, Surrey
Printed and bound in Great Britain by
Billing & Sons Ltd, Worcester

Contents

Acknowledgements

First a very special thank you to Katie O'Hara without whose generous help the first part of this book could not have been written.

Grateful thanks to the Brooke family, Charlie Micklen, George and Olive Manley, and Joss Hanbury for their stories about Gossip. To the 'technicians' Lesley Gowers who shaped script into book and to John Beaton for bringing together the later stages. To Lady Doreen Prior-Palmer for kindly reading the original script and advising in the text.

And lastly a warm thank-you to the many others who were involved at one time or another in Gossip's life and have contributed their own reminiscences.

1 Teething Troubles

In the range of the Wicklow mountains that run in a north-west, south-east direction, below Dublin, towards the eastern coast of Ireland, stands Lugnoquilla, famed as the second highest mountain in Ireland. Below the mountain sprawl emerald-green fields divided by soft grey-stone walls that weave in a drunken line through plots of luscious spring grass.

On 30th May, 1968, in one such field, a dark-brown thoroughbred colt was struggling to his feet, eager to glimpse his first sight of the world. The foal's grey thoroughbred mother proudly watched her son take his initial wobbly steps. She was called Jut Gold, and one of her most famous ancestors was The Tetrarch, otherwise known as Spotted Wonder because of his coat, which was grey with white patches. In 1913 The Tetrarch was one of the fastest two-year-olds alive and was unbeaten in seven starts.

Jut Gold herself had never raced. She was kept as a brood mare by George Manley, one of Ireland's many part-time breeders. This activity he fitted into his life of mixed farming, of sheep, cattle and tillage.

For a thoroughbred, Jut Gold had an amenable, friendly temperament. One little quirk she indulged was to gallop three or four laps around her field when anyone approached to catch her. She always insisted on a quick fling of freedom, before stopping in the centre of the field and allowing the headcollar to be slipped over her head.

The colt's sire, Ardfert, was owned by George's father-in-law and stood at the Goldenfort Stud, a few miles away. Ardfert, a thoroughbred bay stallion, had raced and won at Phoenix Park in Dublin as a three-year-old before being turned to stud duties. Relations on his side included an

English mother and grandmother, who were both foaled in France. Mirabile II, his grandmother, had won two races in France and was placed ten times on the flat.

Ardfert was a strong-charactered horse whose progeny included several show-jumpers. He had a wily temperament, demonstrated aptly one day when he nearly bit off his owner's fingers whilst being patted on the nose.

Most of Jut Gold's foals were to be destined for National Hunt yards and, from his breeding, it seemed this latest arrival would follow a similar career.

But during the first year of the foal's life, George sometimes wondered just what his mare had produced. He soon realised that he had one of the toughest-ever yearlings on his hands. Clearly the foal had inherited much of his father's artful character. He had an astonishingly fast brain and fired a ceaseless battery of tricks on the unsuspecting George and his wife, Olive.

Every time George entered the stable, he was presented with the furry tail of the foal's rear end, as the suspicious youngster activated his guard whenever someone appeared in his box. The foal was just playing games, but George felt he never could quite trust the foal not to kick out at him. As a result, it often took George over an hour merely to catch the colt in the stable.

Olive Manley also became the target for practical jokes, but one day *she* succeeded in having the last laugh. On this occasion Olive went out to the field to feed him, and the youngster came running straight at her, mouth open. Olive wasn't going to wait for the onslaught. In her hand she held a bucket, which the youngster probably thought contained feed, and he was in a hurry for his meal. Olive didn't hesitate. She flung the contents – a gallon of water – over the youngster's head and fled from the field.

Equine friends also tried to teach the colt a lesson. After he had been weaned he shared a field with an elderly donkey. The poor donkey was chivvied and bullied unmercifully all day long. Eventually his long-suffering companion was forced to take refuge under some bushes. He then retaliated by sneaking out from his retreat and, when the chance arose, grabbing hold of the colt's tail when the youngster wasn't looking. The tail was soon reduced to little more than a few chewed tufts.

During the following summer of 1969, the colt was prepared for the August sales at Ballsbridge, Dublin, held by Goffs, Ireland's best-known bloodstock auctioneers. Teaching the colt to lead in-hand, George found nearly impossible. Frequently he was involved in sparring sessions as a foreleg suddenly shot up over the lead-rope in an attempt to knock George over.

However, despite the yearling's naughtiness and tufted tail, he was a good-looking animal with strong, clean limbs and George was confident of receiving a good price at the sales.

The yearling was bought for 330 guineas, by a Mr J. Riordan, but details of the youngster's life over the next two years have proved elusive. During that time he was sold on privately to a Mr Daniel Malony.

In August 1971, Lot 346 at the Ballsbridge Sales turns out to be the same colt, now an unbroken three-year-old.

As he was led round the sales ring, he was noticed by Omagh horse dealer, John Chambers. John's chief interest lay in finding suitable horses for show-jumping. He was impressed with the colt's looks and strong, compact body. The horse became his for 400 guineas.

A few hours later John was convinced he had made a horrible mistake. So much so that he even tried unsuccessfully to stop his cheque. The horse was a monster. John had never encountered such a vicious bad-tempered animal in his life. When John went to inspect his new purchase in the stable, the horse flew at him as he poked his head over the half door, and he only narrowly escaped being boxed on the nose by flailing forefeet.

John wasn't even very sure of how he was going to transport the colt home, as nobody could catch him in the stable – those that were brave enough to try. In the end John had to leave the horse at Ballsbridge overnight. The next day he backed a horsebox up to the stable door and, helped by several friends, herded the colt onto the lorry, as one might a flock of sheep. He then set off over the border to Omagh.

The horse's manners did not improve at his new home. John considered him too dangerous to be looked after by girl grooms, so only men dealt with him. Through the autumn John began the far from easy task of breaking the horse in. Putting a blanket on, caused the horse to cavort around his stable in a series of electrifying bucks. John would wait ten or fifteen minutes before attempting to put on and tighten up the roller, knowing otherwise the horse would go berserk.

Introducing the three-year-old to saddle, bridle and then a rider, proved less of a battle than John imagined. The saddling process took time and patience, in order to avoid explosions whilst the girth was being tightened. Surprisingly, John came up against little resistance when the time came to leg a rider aboard. But another obstacle presented itself instead, in that the youngster refused to turn to the right. John deduced one possible theory: perhaps the horse had been lunged too much on one rein, as can often happen in racing yards. Consequently, especially in a young animal, muscles might have developed rapidly on one side and produced resistance and stiffness on the other. And habits picked up so young are very hard to rectify.

As the days shortened into winter the horse's temperament in the stable became no easier. The mutual feeling of mistrust never relaxed between the horse and his keepers. The youngster was always on his guard, suspicious of any noise or movement. He was totally unpredictable, and nobody trusted him enough to think they might not be bitten or kicked whenever they entered his stable.

As the youngster's education progressed, John knew it was time he found a name for his latest acquisition. Over the months nothing obvious had come to mind other than a string of unprintable oaths. Then, talking to someone on the 'phone one day, John happened to glance up at a big silver cup sitting on his sideboard. It had been won by his father three years in succession, 1926, 1927 and 1928, on a show horse called Village Gossip.

'Then, that's who he'll be,' decided John. It was a likeable name, in contrast to the youngster's character, but maybe, John mused, one day the new Gossip would live up to the standard his father's horse had attained. Though considering the new Gossip's nightmarish temperament, John was distinctly dubious of the horse achieving anything other than notoriety.

So, as 1972 arrived, Gossip at last had an identity though it bore little relationship to that of his famous predecessor.

As part of his schooling, John hunted Gossip lightly through January and February, and was pleasantly surprised to find a much more co-operative horse. He was very hard to hold, but was a happier person when faced with an expanse of green turf or an inviting hedge than ever he was when hacking or schooling at home. He proved a brave horse across country, jumping anything John asked of him.

It wasn't a hunter John wanted though, but a show-jumper. So often weekends were taken up competing at various indoor jumping shows in the locality. One venue for these shows was at Ashbrook Equestrian Centre, home of the Viscount and Viscountess Brookeborough. Lord Brookeborough had show-jumped to international level in the fifties, and only just missed selection for the Helsinki Olympics in 1952 when his horse went lame in the final days of training. Lady Brookeborough's expertise lay in her skill with young horses. An exceptionally talented rider, her brilliance was unsurpassed in the reformation of seemingly intractable animals.

At Ashbrooke, the Brookeboroughs bought and sold horses for almost every facet of equine sport. Their five children all rode, and their second son, Christopher Brooke, had won the Junior Three-Day Event Championship in Germany in 1971, on the brilliant dun 15hh horse, Olive Oyl.

Ashbrooke was also, to an extent, a riding school. Lady Brookeborough gave lessons and was backed up by other qualified teaching staff.

Gossip's debut to his competitive career was not auspicious. At the Ashbrooke shows he wasted everybody's time by napping, either in the middle of a round or at the beginning by refusing to cross the start line. At one show Gossip was being so impossible that John had no alternative but to accept a lead over the entire course.

Because of the havoc he was creating, Lady Brookeborough

could not help but notice Gossip. She was quickly aware that there was something special about his jump, but otherwise there was little to like about him. The horse had one of the nastiest, irascible tempers Lady Brookeborough had come across, which even his good looks could not dismiss.

As the weather softened into spring, John took Gossip to outdoor shows. They still had fights when Gossip napped, particularly if the course started on the right rein or passed close to the collecting ring. But Gossip did jump clear on several occasions and it was rare that he ever stopped in front of a fence, but John could sense that the horse was not really enjoying life as a show-jumper.

Then, just for fun, John took Gossip to the local point-to-point course, the day after a meet had been held, and schooled him around the inviting brush fences. John was astounded at the change of character. Gossip pricked his ears and flew across the turf, revelling in his own speed and power.

Gossip's obvious delight at this new form of exercise underlined the point all too clearly to John. Gossip was never going to enjoy show-jumping and consequently would probably never be any good at it. The point-to-point or National Hunt scene now looked the logical goal for utilising Gossip's talents.

So, for the fourth time in four years, Gossip was back on the market. Once again Gossip headed for Dublin, but this time not to the sales. Instead John entered him for the Dublin Horse Show.

Held annually in August this show is one of the highlights of the equestrian calendar. Also held at Ballsbridge, it is not unlike a sale because the vast gathering of competitors and enthusiasts from the showing and jumping worlds, both from Ireland and abroad, creates a buoyant market. John was fairly confident of finding a buyer.

To show Gossip off to the public, John had had to enter him in a showing class as Gossip had not qualified for any of the jumping competitions. But Gossip had no intention of being paraded for all the world to see. As the class began to file into the ring Gossip napped and adamantly refused to follow the other horses: they were walking round the arena on the right rein.

The possibility of finding a purchaser now looked about as likely as rain in the desert. Who on earth would buy a horse that would not even follow others into the ring?

But there was someone who had been watching Gossip's antics in the collecting ring, and with more than just passing interest. That person was Lady Brookeborough.

She offered John a price that initially he was reluctant to consider, wanting at least to receive his initial purchase price.

But, not surprisingly, no other offers were forthcoming, so John decided he might be wiser to have the horse taken off his yard before he ran into more problems.

Gossip changed hands again and was delivered to Ashbrooke in County Fermanagh.

His reputation had already preceded him. As he was led off the horsebox in the yard at Ashbrooke the staff and pupils uttered wails of horror and protest. But Lady Brookeborough told them with a wry smile that she had bought him for no other reason than that she knew he could jump, and she thought she might learn something from him.

But for the first few months of that autumn, it was Gossip who learnt the most. He was long-reined in the indoor school every day. Lady Brookeborough's first aim was to encourage Gossip to move forward obediently and willingly, a request he was very loath to comply with unless he was heading in the direction of home. For this reason he was always worked in the indoor school, where he was hemmed in by four walls. His work was carried out without the hindrance of a rider on his back, so there was no excuse for him to put up any evasions.

In a matter of weeks Gossip was responding agreeably to the long-reins, and Lady Brookeborough decided to try riding him outside. She rode him into a field in front of the house. Every time Gossip passed the gate he napped, and the more Lady Brookeborough worked him the worse he became. So it was back to the school and the long-reins. It was nearly Christmas before Gossip was to have a rider on his back again and be permitted to work outside.

In December, Lady Brookeborough deemed it was time to put a rider onto Gossip whilst he was on the lunge. This dubious honour was allotted to the eldest daughter, Juliana.

Gossip behaved so beautifully that it wasn't long before Juliana tried working him off the lunge. This had mixed success. Some days Gossip was angelic. On others Juliana would be in tears of frustration, as Gossip reverted to napping and refusing to co-operate. Juliana once spent four hours trying to persuade him to trot a right-handed circle inside four poles lying on the ground. Sometimes, to try and wear him out, she would trot him for miles across harrowed fields, but the exercise had little effect on his seemingly bottomless stamina. When these arguments occurred, out would come the lunge reins and lunge whip, and Gossip would go back to endless circles in the school.

One aid Gossip did listen to and respect above all others was the voice. He had become sub-consciously attuned to Lady Brookeborough over the months she had worked him from the ground, when all the commands had been vocal. He gradually became more responsive to the voice, declining to listen to the legs or reins.

By February 1973, Juliana, preoccupied with marriage plans, thankfully handed over Gossip to brother Alan.

Cheerfully ignorant of what might happen, Alan rode Gossip at the horse's introduction to cross-country competition – a hunter trial. Gossip was diabolical. Taking an iron-like hold on the right rein, Gossip ran past almost every fence he was presented at and galloped at break-neck speed between them.

The day after the competition, a seething Alan took Gossip to one of the fields adjoining the yard at Ashbrooke. There he tried to break the unyielding hold Gossip had on the right rein. For threequarters of an hour that morning, the sound of drumming hoof-beats could be heard coming from the field behind the stables. The tempo of the pounding never slowed, and, in alarm, someone went to check Alan was still on board. At length a white and exhausted Alan reappeared in the yard accompanied by a steaming, foaming Gossip. The defiant look in Gossip's eyes said it all. He was put back in his stable and ignored for the rest of the day.

Soon after this escapade, Gossip produced a large splint on his off (right) foreleg, and every time he knocked it he went lame. So he was turned out for a rest with several other horses in a field, three or four miles down the road, probably to the silent relief of those who had been riding or looking after him.

For a while Gossip was virtually forgotten. In fact he was allowed to languish at grass long after the splint had settled, principally because nobody could catch him. The other horses were occasionally caught and used for lessons, but Gossip kept well clear of any humans.

Then – and this was becoming an annual event in Gossip's life – an opportunity arose in early September for Lady Brookeborough to sell Gossip.

An army friend, Richard Coghlan, rang up to enquire whether the Brookeboroughs had a thoroughbred horse suitable for hunting.

Lady Brookeborough felt she should not miss this chance to sell Gossip. He was an impossibly problematic horse and took up so much of her valuable time when he was in work. Moreover, he had yet to show that he would ever be co-operative enough to be successful in the competitive field, in which case hunting or point-to-pointing seemed the only alternative solution.

Richard Coghlan was going to be at a show the Brooke-boroughs were attending with several horses in two days' time. So the day before the show, six people made their way down to Gossip's field and spent the entire afternoon trying to catch him.

Gossip was horrified at the prospect of losing his freedom, and hid behind his equine friends so nobody could reach him. By tea-time his would-be captors were worn out from trekking after him around the field. They tried a different tactic. Herding all the horses into the narrow funnel of land running up to the gate, they released the horses, one by one, into the field behind them, until only Gossip was left in the funnel. He was driven into a corner and, at last, someone managed to put a headcollar over his ears. On the long walk back to Ashbrooke four people 'whipped-in' behind him, as Gossip would grudgingly walk a few steps, then halt, staring about at the scenery, totally indifferent to the situation, and refuse to budge until he was vigorously encouraged from the rear.

The following morning a ragged unkempt Gossip was loaded onto the horsebox, alongside spruced equine companions. Richard Coghlan was to try him out at the showground.

Despite his long sojourn in the field, Gossip behaved well for Richard, who appreciated the sensitivities of thoroughbreds. He rode him intelligently, with a light rein, and allowed Gossip's humping back to relax and settle before testing his paces.

Feeling no undue pressure or tension, which frequently provoked a nap, Gossip stayed obligingly calm, and his annual change of residence looked certain when Richard agreed to buy him subject to a routine veterinary inspection.

Gossip failed the vet. The report indicated that Gossip had an irregular heart-beat, which, although not a major worry, was enough to put Richard off the purchase of a horse destined for the rigours of the hunting field.

Lady Brookeborough was in despair. Gossip was practically unridable, utterly impossible to look after and, now, totally unsalable. The thought of having a horse in the yard with a suspect heart problem was extremely unnerving and brought forth one over-riding conclusion: Gossip would have to go. But how? and where to? were harder to answer. In one moment of complete indecision and despair there were even mutterings of sending him to the meat-man, a dreadful thought which was never seriously considered; but meanwhile nobody could come up with any solutions to Gossip's future.

While the Brookeboroughs debated over his fate, Gossip was incorporated back into life at Ashbrooke. He was being looked after by Billy Stevenson, who was then head lad. But inevitably, with Gossip's inherent dislike and suspicion of men, he and Billy were hardly the best of friends. Gossip was still a terror in the stable and just as difficult to catch. Billy found the only answer was to creep into Gossip's stable and grab hold of the front of his rug. Then the secret was to hang on tight while Gossip spun round the stable, trying to rid himself of the offending object apparently glued to the front of his rug. If Billy hung on long enough, Gossip would eventually stop revolving and succumb to being caught.

Gossip was always wary of anyone who came into his stable, and Billy's method of catching was the only one which seemed to work. The tiresome, frustrating tasks involved in looking after Gossip, who kicked continuously when being groomed or saddled, and lunged at anyone who entered his box, did not endear him to those around him, least of all Billy who had to cope with him every day.

One morning Billy was standing outside the feed-shed, grumbling to a friend about the difficulties of looking after Gossip. He was overheard by a young Irish girl named Katie O'Hara, who had come to Ashbrooke in February to help out for a few weeks and had somehow ended up staying indefinitely.

Katie listened to Billy's justifiable complaints but immediately felt sorry for Gossip. Nobody liked the little black horse, but Katie was one of those people whose kind heart would always support the underdog.

She poked her head out of the feed-shed, 'OK, Billy,' she said, 'I'll do Gossip for you. I don't mind him.'

It was the beginning of Gossip's reformation.

2 Metamorphosis

Two years previously, Katie O'Hara had spent six months at Ashbrooke studying for and passing her BHSAI exam. She had then adopted a radical change of life-style and become an au pair, taking jobs in Europe and Morocco. On her return from foreign lands she reapplied to Ashbrooke and became part of the teaching staff.

Katie has a delightfully 'Irish', happy-go-lucky attitude to life. She rarely becomes cross or bad-tempered and nearly always has a broad smile on her face. With horses she is calm and patient, always ready to give them as much time as they need. Discovering what makes each horse tick she finds fascinating and absorbing.

When Katie took over Gossip she soon discovered that under his tough, aggressive outer shell there hid a very, very frightened person. Drawing possible conclusions, Katie felt that Gossip must have projected such a fearsome image as a foal that, naturally, people involved with him had become cautious and on their guard. Sensing their nervousness, Gossip himself had become wary, and gradual feelings of mistrust had steadily grown on both sides. As Gossip had come up against discipline and authority, his strong natural cheek had turned into rebellion, and this, no doubt, had been counteracted by strong reprimands from his teachers. Tempers and tensions had spiralled and Gossip had increasingly reacted with more ferocious defence weapons in the form of teeth and heels, hiding his real self behind an ever-thickening wall of aggression.

Slowly and quietly, Katie began to learn about Gossip. She talked to him when mucking out his box or when grooming him, and in spare moments she sat in his stable and made a fuss of him, giving him time to become acquainted with yet another stranger.

At first there was little change. Gossip continued to gnash his teeth and swing his bottom to the door, lifting a hind leg threateningly as she entered. Katie ignored his threats. One of the vital missing ingredients in Gossip's make-up was trust, and Katie knew she had to make the first move to instil it. To begin with, Gossip was puzzled. The expected rebuke never came. Instead, this strange person carried on as though he had done nothing. Gossip could not understand it. Awakening interest stirred inside him; perhaps this was not just another person against whom he would have to defend himself.

Soon Gossip recognised Katie's voice, his ears flicking forward when he heard the familiar tone. Affection was another sadly elusive ingredient in Gossip's life, but under Katie's care he really began to believe his unhappy days were past. Sometimes Katie would rush into his stable at odd moments to give him a huge bear hug. His instant reaction would be to flatten his ears and glare at her furiously, then his chameleon character would alter as she flung her arms around his neck. His ears would come forward and his soft nose would seek out her body to say hello. Their mutual trust deepened and Katie would quite happily walk up to Gossip's backside and give it a hug, knowing he would never kick her, although the ingrained habit of swinging his quarters towards the door, *whoever* entered, Gossip could never quite discard.

Nobody had made any further decisions about Gossip's future and, indeed, it seemed he had almost been forgotten. So Katie started to ride him. Or rather she used him as a mode of transport, riding him while teaching in the school, escorting hacks or demonstrating to the students how to do hillwork etc. Gossip relaxed, finding he had nothing to fight; Katie's attention was always primarily directed at whomever she was teaching and he began to enjoy his daily exercise.

As the autumn days of 1973 disappeared, Katie became more wrapped up in Gossip. When there was time she took him for long hacks in the surrounding countryside. Gossip was happy and at ease on the loose rein that Katie always gave him. She popped him over small natural fences, and they scrambled up and down banks and over ditches. Gossip was learning that life could be fun – if he allowed it to be so.

So quick-thinking and intelligent was Gossip's mind that he and Katie were soon able to join in more serious cross-country schooling sessions under Lady Brookeborough, tackling the various man-made fences at Ashbrooke. Another trait Gossip would never discard was his nap, and initially he would only jump with other horses around or in front of him. He attacked his fences, always rather faster than was necessary, pulling hard. Katie had a notion that galloping frightened Gossip. The speed of the pace alarmed him and brought out his natural instincts to run away from pressures and possible danger. In fact, Gossip was so concerned over the galloping that the fences never bothered him. In time, he developed his own unique style of jumping, by galloping flat out into a fence, shortening and slowing himself up only a couple of strides out to judge the take-off point, flying over the obstacle, then continuing at the same break-neck pace.

Still without any definite plans for his future, Lady Brookeborough resumed her interest in Gossip now that he was back in full work. Lady Brookeborough was the only person Gossip had absolute respect for, and he would obey her without question. She continued his work on the long reins, with which Gossip was at his best. He had no rider to worry about so his concentration was entirely on Lady Brookeborough in the centre of the circle. She imbued in him such strong feelings of confidence, security and trust that Gossip never wanted to deny her requests. Lady Brookeborough had superb judgment in knowing just *when* to ask Gossip to perform a certain movement or to introduce a new one. Before, people had asked him for obedience but at the wrong moment, or had asked him too many difficult questions too soon. Gossip had become so nervous and frightened that finally he said, 'No, I won't.'

Brick by brick, Lady Brookeborough and Katie carefully built up Gossip's confidence and trust in the human race. The change they wrought was little short of a miracle.

As his education progressed, Katie took Gossip to informal shows and events if there happened to be a space in the horsebox that was going from Ashbrooke. Katie always rode him. No one else wanted to. He could still be extremely stubborn and frequently napped when Katie tried to ride out of the yard on him. Katie would then have to yell for someone to chase after him with a lunge whip, as he would refuse point blank to move in any direction but backwards.

In early November, Gossip suffered a painful and needlessly distressing experience that did little to promote and engender any sort of trust in humans.

The vet was called to Ashbrooke for the removal of some wolf teeth from three horses, one of whom was Gossip. The vet decided that the easiest way to treat Gossip was to anaesthetise him. The operation was carried out in the indoor school. As Gossip sank to his knees and collapsed onto his side, Katie realised to her horror that the anaesthetic was having a strange effect on him. Gossip started to shake from head to foot and sweat poured off him in torrents. And this was only the overture. The supposedly simple operation took two hours to perform. The vet had to saw through bone, and at the end of it all, it was discovered he had removed the wrong teeth. He had taken out the tushes (teeth that lie half way between the incisors and where wolf teeth appear, which is in front of the molars), which rarely cause any problems. No one could fathom what went wrong. Whether the vet thought he was meant to take out the tushes or whether it was a genuine, but ghastly, mistake, nobody was quite sure. Even odder, he took the tushes out of the second horse too, but on the third one, he extracted the wolf teeth.

For Gossip, it was like waking up to a nightmare. As he struggled to his feet in the school, he was temporarily blinded, his eyes gummed up with sweat and dirt from the floor. His mouth was agonisingly painful and swelling rapidly from the bruising of the extractions. For a week he was unable to eat properly, and Katie had to syringe out the cavities daily to keep them clean. It was over a fortnight before Gossip was feeling well enough to be worked again, and then only on the lunge from a headcollar to allow maximum time for his mouth to heal.

When Katie was able to ride him again, she encountered

another problem. Gossip displayed a marked aversion to plastic bags. His horror of them was provoked when he caught sight of an empty fertiliser bag wedged in the side of the indoor school where Katie was working him. He refused to go anywhere near it. In an effort to cure him, Katie placed a plastic bag under his hay manger in his stable, in the hopes he would ignore the bag in his desire to eat. In fury, Gossip turned his bottom on his hay and stopped eating. After twenty-four hours Katie gave in and removed the offending object.

On Christmas Eve, Katie took Goose, as she nicknamed Gossip, to her parents' home, ninety minutes' drive away, over the border of County Sligo, for the seasonal holiday. On Boxing Day they both went hunting. Katie was unaware that Gossip had hunted with John Chambers and she was prepared for all sorts of explosions when Gossip first sighted hounds. She was most surprised when Gossip behaved with far more maturity than she was expecting. He was more upset with the other horses swirling around him than he was with hounds' presence. Luckily it was a small field of only thirty mounted followers. Katie quickly found he was happiest if kept in front and a little apart from the others. He pulled and fought most of the day, but jumped everything and 'galloped fabulously!', Katie wrote joyfully in her diary that night.

Katie hunted him a second time a week later, accompanied by sister Caroline mounted on another Ashbrooke horse. Katie kept Gossip in front the entire day, and by evening, as they were backing home, Caroline was green with envy at the ride Gossip had given Katie. This time, Gossip was far more settled and confident and ballooned over every fence with scope and power to spare.

Back at Ashbrooke, in the new year, Gossip began 1974 with star billing. Lady Brookeborough gave a lesson in the indoor school for the benefit of forty-five tourists from all over the world who were visiting Northern Ireland. Gossip behaved impeccably as lead horse, and Katie was thrilled at the way he coped with a big jumping grid at the end of the session. Several of the audience took photos, and later Katie was presented with one of herself and Gossip. It was probably Gossip's first photo since he was a yearling.

At every opportunity Katie show-jumped Gossip, mostly at the indoor shows at Ashbrooke, and kept up a schooling programme under the supervision of and with help from Lady Brookeborough. By February, Gossip had more or less adopted the same training plan as the established event horses at Ashbrooke, but still nobody had voiced any thoughts on the six-year-old's future.

Then one day near the end of the month, Lord Brookeborough mentioned to Katie that he was making plans for a trip to England in May, as Melinda, the second daughter, was eligible to ride in the National Junior Trial at the Tidworth three-day event. Melinda was to ride the family hero, Olive Oyl, now into his teens but proving as brilliant as ever. Lord Brookeborough then came to the reason for his comment. As the horsebox was going to England, he thought they might as well take another horse along, so how would Katie like to take Gossip to compete in one of the adult sections? Katie, having absolutely no idea of what she was letting herself in for, agreed quite happily. The fact that Katie and Gossip had never competed in a one-day event, let alone contemplated a three-day one, was not considered a matter of great significance. Lord Brookeborough would not have made the suggestion if he had thought the challenge was beyond their capabilities, and Katie was quite content to fit in with his plans and look upon it as a big adventure.

Qualifications might have proved a tricky hurdle to overcome, but in those days, they were minimal. After a few 'phone calls Lord Brookeborough discovered that Katie and Gossip's entry would be accepted if the pair could satisfy the Irish Horse Trials Committee that they had some chance of completing the course at Tidworth. To do that it was advised that they should complete at least one course that spring of intermediate standard.

There was no time to be wasted. As a blustery March arrived, Gossip embarked on his eventing career.

But first Lady Brookeborough decided that the time had come to cure another of Gossip's problems and one which was becoming rather destructive. Whenever Gossip was loaded into a horsebox, or trailer, he spent most of the journey kicking at the partitions, seemingly for no other reason than to annoy his fellow passengers, both human and equine. His tattooing feet were also inflicting considerable damage to the sides of the partitions, and Lady Brookeborough thought if she did not find a solution there would be nothing left of the horsebox, now that Gossip would be travelling a great deal.

Lady Brookeborough devised two hobbles comprising two leather straps lined with thick felt. Attached to each was a short chain. The straps were buckled round Gossip's hind pasterns and the chains clipped to a ring on the floor of the horsebox. Gossip accepted the hobbles surprisingly well and did not struggle against them. Lady Brookeborough also found another use for one of them when Gossip was stabled. Gossip used to kick out at the walls with his off hind, again for no particular reason, but the resulting concussion was making the joint on that leg quite severely swollen. If he wore one of the hobbles, with the chain swinging loose, the chain would smack against his leg when he lashed out, and he soon dropped the habit.

On March 29th, Katie and Gossip competed in their first ever one-day event, at novice level.

Gossip was in a very bad temper that day and refused to go forward at all, until he sulkily gave in to Katie's patient wheedling. He was extremely suspicious of the dressage arenas, having never seen the white boards before. As he strutted tensely through the movements, Katie could only sit motionless, asking no more than a change of direction or pace, for fear of snapping the hair-line of communication they had between them.

But his cross-country round wiped out the tantrums of the morning. 'Fantastic!' was Katie's favourite and only word to describe Gossip's abilities in this phase. Even the commentator was impressed and enthused over the loudspeaker in an Irish brogue, 'This is Grand National speed!' as Gossip sped round the course.

Gossip still found galloping an unnerving pace, and when he was allowed to gallop he could not really understand why and must have felt there was something to run from. He hardly seemed to notice the fences and was becoming adept at chipping in a couple of flurried strides before take-off, to balance himself. He did not seriously frighten Katie, as she was coming to trust his lightning judgment – not that she really had any choice: Gossip was virtually uncontrollable. He pulled so hard that Katie could do little more than steer.

Despite his bad dressage Gossip finished third and helped set a good first impression in the eyes of the Irish Horse Trials Committee.

Katie and Gossip completed their required intermediate event a month later. Gossip was feeling very fresh, despite hours of lungeing in a chambon and side-reins, and performed a bubbly test. The course was big but, again, Gossip barely registered the fences' existence. Although unplaced, nobody had any worries that he would not cope at Tidworth.

Competing in a three-day event requires a much higher level of fitness than a one-day competition. So Katie and Gossip spent April and early May walking and trotting up mountainous hills and cantering around vast fields. Katie never knew if Gossip was going to bolt when she did his canter work. It was a considerable feat to maintain a trot round the perimeter of a field. 'He was a real nightmare to ride then,' says Katie. 'An absolute brat! I never knew what he might do, but if he ever decided to go, then there would have been nothing I could have done about it.'

In the middle of May, Gossip, along with Olive Oyl, set sail for Tidworth, a small town on the edge of Salisbury Plain. The course ran over open farmland, sandwiched between the Plain and the town. Tidworth is better known as home to a large army garrison, and the troops stationed there played a big part in helping to run the trials.

Katie's first somewhat ambiguous impression of the Tidworth course was that it was big, boring and difficult. The second time she walked the course, she was grateful for help and advice from a rider who had won her first Badminton the year before on Be Fair. Lucinda Prior-Palmer was down to ride at Tidworth on her second string, Wideawake.

The Brookeboroughs had originally met the Prior-Palmer family in 1971 in Wesel, Germany. Lucinda had been a member, with Chris Brooke, of the victorious Junior British Team, when Chris had claimed the individual title.

Before Katie could centre all her thoughts on the cross country, there was still the dressage phase to be completed, and Katie deflected her concentration onto Gossip's flatwork. On the day prior to his test, she lunged him for up to an hour or more before she rode him, to loosen any tensions and fidgets he might be feeling. Gossip also relaxed far better mentally when there was no rider on his back.

On the day of his test, which was timed for 3.50 pm, Katie began lungeing him at 7.30 in the morning. After nearly two hours of circles, Gossip was put back in his stable and Katie plaited and groomed him. By 1.30 Gossip was back on the lunge and being worked as near to the dressage arenas as possible.

Gossip tried his hardest throughout the test. 'And for him, he was very relaxed,' enthused a delighted Katie, pleased that their hard work had paid off, even if the mark of 78.5 did not quite reflect their feelings. His score left him thirtieth in a field of fifty which was perfectly respectable for a horse who had never seen dressage boards two months ago.

All the best-laid plans can go astray, but on cross-country day Katie's went wrong before she had even mounted. Weighing out at the start of the first set of roads and tracks, phase A, Katie was in a flap when the scales showed she was carrying insufficient lead to make up the minimum weight requirement of 11 stone 11 pounds. Time was running short and a fidgeting Gossip still had to be saddled. The ever-resourceful Brooke family sprang into action. Jane Bullen's horse had just completed phase D, the cross country, but had unhappily collapsed in the official vet Box. The Brookes advanced in a rush upon the rider and helpers. Horribly embarrassed at the awkwardness of this situation, they explained their predicament. Pieces of lead were quickly removed from the luckless horse's weightcloth and shoved into Katie's. The saddle was hurled onto Gossip, and a bevy of fingers snatched at girth and breastplate buckles to strap them into place. Katie was bundled aboard and with no more than seconds to spare, they presented themselves at the start.

Gossip was very confused. His perplexity increased as he set off on phase A – there wasn't a fence in sight. He yanked and tugged at the reins, far too agitated to settle. Katie came in late off this phase, to be met by a mass of Brookes, who were beginning to wonder where she was.

'Right, Katie, shorten up your leathers,' advised Lady Brookeborough. Katie, for a minute, looked puzzled. It hadn't occurred to her that maybe she should ride phase B, the steeplechase, with shorter stirrups, which would make it easier to ride at speed over fences. Katie pulled at her stirrup leather and found she was already on the top hole.

'Thirty seconds, number 121,' called out the starting steward to Katie.

'Oh help. Leather punch, please!' screeched Katie. Brookes scattered and grabbed at the bucket of spare equipment. Someone seized the punch, and then two people tried to keep a whirling Gossip still whilst a third struggled to punch extra holes, at the same time, keeping clear of Gossip's far-reaching cow-kicks.

'121 to the start, please.' Katie forced the tongue of the buckle into the holes and snatched at a fistful of reins. The flurry of human activity ebbed away from Gossip as he cavorted towards the start.

On the word 'Go!', Gossip took off like a bullet from a gun and hurtled round the first circuit. On the second circuit, he was even faster. Katie, having lost all semblance of control, realised the steering wasn't answering either. As the third fence loomed up again, she saw that she was approaching wide, to the left of it. All she could do was to change her whip into her left hand. Too late. They shot past the fence, well outside the penalty zone, like a missile that had veered off target.

Katie hauled Gossip in a circle and set him back on course. They sailed over fence three and completed the rest of the circuit without mishap. Despite his brief detour, Gossip had collected only 4.5 time faults as he had been so fast. But Katie had to let him walk a good distance along phase C, the second set of roads and tracks, as he was very blown and needed time to regain his breath. When he recovered, Katie glanced at her watch and realised they were going to be late again, so she had to canter the last part of phase C to the compulsory ten-minute halt Box.

Gossip, still rather confused at the proceedings, stared about him whilst he was washed down and refreshed before phase D. Remounting, Katie had to be legged up from somewhere near Gossip's head to avoid his cow-kicks, which had incredible range.

All his energies had returned and he rocketed out of the start box of phase D, pulling hard. At the third fence, the Bourne crossing – a hefty pole over a wide, water-filled ditch – Gossip put in an enormous leap when Katie tapped him with her whip to ensure he made the spread. Over the rest of the course, he was superb, too fast as usual, but he never gave Katie a moment's doubt or hesitation. After every fence, Katie gave him a reassuring pat as he sped away to the next jump with ever-increasing confidence.

At the end of the day Gossip had moved up to fifteenth place, and an amazed Katie was over-joyed with her clever Goose. It was their third ever cross-country.

Warming up for the show-jumping the following afternoon, Katie could sense Gossip feeling worried and uncomfortable with this phase, as John Chambers had felt two years earlier.

He was nervous as he entered the arena, but nevertheless managed to jump clear and even moved up two places to thirteenth. Katie attributed his nerves to the crowd of spectators; certainly the fences themselves held no fears.

The Brookeboroughs and Katie were delighted with Gossip's performance. It was hard to believe that the same horse had been lounging in a field twelve months earlier, unwanted and unloved and with a large questionmark hanging over his future.

On returning to Ireland, Gossip was given a long holiday and he spent much of the summer growing fat and sleek, whiling away hot lazy days in the verdant paddocks around Ashbrooke.

In August he was brought back into work. He was in such high spirits, he began bucking in his stable, so Katie resorted to several days of lungeing before climbing on to his back.

The first event of that autumn was not a success. Katie and

some members of the Brooke family who were competing, all managed to miss out a fence when they walked the course. They justifiably received a strong verbal rocket from Lady Brookeborough, furious at such incompetence, because each of them when they rode round was eliminated. The following weekend, however, all was redeemed when Gossip won his first intermediate.

As the autumn progressed, Gossip's education improved in leaps and bounds due in no small part to Lady Brookeborough's continuing work with the long reins, when Gossip was at his most relaxed, complying instantly with her wishes.

Gossip and Katie also gained much valuable experience over several intermediate one-day events. Always his cross country was brilliant, but his dressage all too often let him down, as he stiffened and hollowed with tension, his head and neck position sometimes resembling that of an obdurate camel. Just occasionally he softened, but he never completely gave to Katie's hand and leg. So his excellent conformation and above-average paces were never given a chance to be shown off to their fullest extent.

At the end of September, Katie took Gossip to Scarva, home of well-known Irish horse dealer, Bill Buller, for the Irish Open and Novice One-Day Event Championships. The course was enormous and there was virtually no difference between the open and novice fences. Katie, who also had a ride in the open class on another Brookeborough horse, succeeded in gaining one of only three clear rounds in that division.

Later in the day the novices were encountering endless problems, faults coming mostly from a bank and rails with a seven-foot drop on the far side. Many people considered Katie was mad to ride Gossip, despite his good showing at Tidworth, which several opinions thought was a fluke. Those who knew Gossip from the past were genuinely concerned that the horse's notorious temperament was so dangerous it could even cause Katie injury. And nobody thought he would come good because of his well-known tendency to nap. At Scarva, John Agnew, one of Ireland's most prominent horse vets, strongly advised Katie to forget the horse. 'A napping horse will always nap,' he warned. 'You'll never get the better of him.'

Gossip must have heard and understood John Agnew's words because he nearly eliminated himself before reaching the first fence. The problem was that the entrance to the horsebox park lay beside the track the horses had to follow from the start to the first jump. As Katie urged Gossip into a canter she could sense 'backward thoughts' in Gossip's mind. He stopped abruptly by the gap and froze, his eyes swirling in their sockets as he sighted the horseboxes. Katie could do nothing but sit and *hope* he might condescend to move. Luck intervened. Juliana just happened to be walking through the gap at that moment. Trying her best to mimic her mother, Juliana commanded, 'Trot on!' Gossip automatically reacted. He dropped his head and trotted off as though he was on the long reins in the school. Katie quickly gathered him up and focused his attention on the approaching fence, giving him no time to realise he had been duped.

Concentrating wholeheartedly on the course, Gossip did not waver again. He jumped outstandingly, dismissing the difficult fences with a professional flourish. He took one of the two second prizes which Katie collected on each of her horses.

The Novice Championships were the highlight of Gossip's autumn season in 1974. He was only six years old and had accumulated an incredible wealth of experience as well as a considerable amount of success, proving the sceptics wrong every step of the way. But despite Gossip's success, there were no ambitious plans for this uniquely talented horse. Katie was very appreciative of the Brookes' generosity in allowing her to continue riding him, when he could have been given to Alan or Chris, who were both more experienced riders. But Lord and Lady Brookeborough rarely considered switching riders and horses unless a combination was having problems. With their own children, who were infrequently at home, it is unlikely that Gossip would have made such rapid progress or been so settled if he'd had a rider that only worked him for a few days or a few weeks at a time. With the added bonus of Katie looking after him as well as riding him, the two had forged a rapport that had improved Gossip's character totally from the vicious, frightened horse that John Chambers had bought. Instead of fear and aggression, these two diverse character traits had been remoulded and blended into tremendous affection for Katie, and a wicked sense of humour. Gossip would use a veil of ferociousness on unsuspecting newcomers to Ashbrooke, to thoroughly alarm, but if they were brave and saw through his charade, Gossip would gradually allow them to make a fuss of him, twining his neck around them in affection, as he always did with Katie.

But no degree of character change was as responsible for his early successes as was his training from Lady Brookeborough, who was the chief instigator of Gossip's achievements, Gossip needed someone who had the knowledge of where to start unravelling the tangled net in which he had become ensnarled during the first years of his life. Gossip, through Lady Brookeborough's quiet yet positive authority, gained the self-confidence and calmness to carry out whatever she asked without becoming worried or panicky and resorting to his bolt-hole of napping.

It was on such a platform of security and assurance that Gossip entered his seventh year in 1975.

3 The Butterfly Emerges

In January, Katie took Gossip on a training course given by Jock Ferrie, team trainer to the Irish three-day-event team. During the course, Katie again met Lucinda who had been invited to give a talk during the weekend. Lucinda, who was joined by her parents, stayed on in Ireland for a few days after the course, as house guests of the Brookeboroughs. The Prior-Palmers showed great interest in the activities at Ashbrooke, and on several occasions Katie found three keen pairs of eyes watching her as she worked Gossip in the school.

Although no one had given any definite indications, there was a silent assumption that Gossip would be aimed again for Tidworth, along with three other horses to be ridden by Chris, Melinda and Paul Hanna, resident 'stable jockey' at Ashbrooke. Alan, whose regiment was stationed in Germany, was also riding and had his horse with him.

Gossip's preparation was taken more seriously this year and followed a rigorous fitness routine. The basis of this programme, which was used on all the event horses at Ashbrooke, was slow cantering in the indoor school, ridden with only a headcollar and reins, no saddle, just a numnah. This method encouraged the horse to completely relax mentally and to stretch and tone up his muscles for the faster work that came later. The horses worked up to as much as four lots of ten-minute canters, interspersed by three-, four- or five-minute walking breaks, or alternatively they would do two lots of twenty minutes' cantering. The work was gradually increased until they were cantering twice a week in the school. The programmes were structured to each individual horse. This method suited Gossip well as even he couldn't be bothered to become excited and pull just cantering round and round the school.

The method also had its advantages in that the fields were often too wet in early spring or frozen from overnight frosts to enable the horses to work on them. But, obviously, the faster work had to be undertaken outside and included in the programme was hillwork, done at walk, trot and canter, up and down varying gradients.

On days when the horses were not cantering, they were schooled on the flat and over jumping grids, they show-jumped, practised cross country and, on certain days, were taken for a quiet hack as a form of light relief.

Gossip's first event that year was at the end of March. To everyone's enormous surprise, Gossip led the intermediate section after the dressage, albeit with a score of seventy. It was a miserable wet day and the proceedings had to be delayed at one stage, it was raining so hard. Katie didn't mind as the downpour encouraged Gossip to drop his head down during his test and so help his marks. He continued to hold his lead throughout the day as horses slithered and battled their way round the waterlogged course, and he won the class.

At the next event, in the third week of April, the ground was even worse after interminable rain, and Katie withdrew Gossip from the competition before the cross country. Tidworth now became a definite date, and loomed up as the next event on the calendar.

In early May, Katie was allowed to try riding Gossip in a gag. Lady Brookeborough did not agree with putting all sorts of ironmongery in horses' mouths, believing that correct schooling should provide the key. But there are exceptions to every rule and Gossip was the exception to this one. Up to now, Katie had ridden him in only a snaffle and drop noseband, with a running martingale for cross country. But, on course, Katie could not hold him, and in spite of his dramatic improvement on the flat he was not becoming any easier. Katie did not want a repeat performance of their tearaway round on the steeplechase, and she was anxious to have some sort of control on the cross country, especially at fences that required an angled approach or a steadier pace. Lady Brookeborough suggested a gag deploying two reins. Katie could then mostly ride off the top, snaffle rein and use the levering stronger action of the bottom rein as a sort of emergency handbrake.

Katie experimented with the gag, combined with a grakle noseband, over some of the cross-country fences at Ashbrooke and was relieved to find she did have a little more say in the matter.

So with the brakes relined Gossip set out on his second visit to England, this time, like his rider, primed with a wealth more experience and knowledge of what was required.

At this Tidworth, Katie's appraisal of the course was that it was big but navigable if she rode using her head. (This last piece of self-analytical information she kept to herself in case she didn't.)

She prepared Gossip for his dressage test in the same way as she had in 1974. Hours of lungeing were interspersed with schooling on the polo grounds, which was where the dressage and show-jumping phases took place.

Gossip was now more at ease and better acquainted with the eventing scene. He settled more readily for his test, though never completely submitting as always there was an under-current of tension. However, his test was a big improvement on his 1974 effort and a mark of 60.8 put him into fourteenth place.

Katie's headlines in her diary for the cross-country day of Tidworth '75 read, 'Boy, oh boy, oh, Epic Day!', though the initial proceedings of that day were far from epic.

The day was cold and wet and the going quickly became churned into slippery mud. Katie wasn't due to start phase A until the afternoon, so in the morning she took the opportunity of walking the course again, watching how the fences were jumping. She was thankful she did, for she saw some bad falls and learnt of possible pitfalls. Even worse, other members of the Brookeborough team were having grave problems. Alan incurred two stops, Paul fell off at the first Bourne crossing, and Chris fell off three times, the third fall causing hilarity among spectators as his horse went *under* the rail spanning the water-filled ditch. Chris's acrobatics, as he grabbed at the rail and clung on like a monkey, gave photographers the shot of the month.

This year there were no panics with the weights, and as Gossip cantered down the first hill of phase A, Katie was congratulating herself on her untroubled progress so far. Next minute, Gossip skidded as he turned on a wet and muddy concrete road. His legs shot from under him and he crashed down onto his side. Katie extricated herself and jumped to her feet, breeches covered in gritty dirt. She clung on to the reins as Gossip struggled to his feet, knowing he would head straight back to the stables if he found himself loose. Anxious not to lose precious seconds, Katie scrambled back into the saddle and hurried on towards phase B. It wasn't until they had nearly reached the steeplechase, when Katie glanced down at her watch, that she saw, to her horror, blood oozing from Gossip's left shoulder. She then noticed that her left elbow was also bleeding.

It had never occurred to her that they might have sustained any injuries from their fall. And to cap her problems, Katie because aware of ominous creakings from her saddle.

'That's it,' thought Katie miserably. 'My saddle is broken, Gossip will be lame and I'll be too stiff to hold him on the cross country.'

The Brookes were waiting for her at the start of the steeplechase. A flustered Katie told them what had happened and that she couldn't go on. What was she to do? Lady Brookeborough swiftly examined Gossip, who was perfectly sound, told Katie not to be so stupid, to ignore what had happened and to keep going. A surge of relief swept through Katie at Lady Brookeborough's positive orders. She pulled herself together and set off on the steeplechase. The course, like last year's, was mostly downhill over huge brush fences. Katie had only slightly more control this time but having learnt her lesson, she changed her stick into her left hand at the start. Gossip finished with 0.8 of a time fault, which that year was the fastest time on the 'chase. Many other competitors were collecting up to 40 time penalties on phase B, the heavy going and steep hill to the finish taking their toll on tired horses.

As Katie and Gossip made their way along phase C, Katie could still hear noises from her saddle. Alan, on his way back to the Box, drove alongside and asked if all was OK. Katie voiced her fears over the possible state of the saddle, so they decided to change it in the Box, in case the tree had been damaged.

Gossip trotted into the Box off phase C sound, much to Katie's relief, thinking he might have stiffened up after the steeplechase. The Brookes descended on Gossip and quickly changed the saddle, strapping Katie's weight-cloth onto the spare, at the same time skilfully avoiding Gossip's hooves, which shot out and round every other second as he cow-kicked.

The starter gave the countdown and they were away. Gossip sped off at a fast, uncontrollable pace over the first few fences. Although the course ran in the opposite direction to the previous year Katie swore Gossip knew exactly where he was going. The gag wasn't helping much and Katie had some dicy moments as Gossip skittered across the combination fences without any perceptible decrease in speed. At the last Bourne crossing where Chris had come unstuck, Gossip launched himself and took off a stride too early, terrifying Katie. Perhaps he remembered the tap he had received in '74 when he jumped it the other way, and he was out to prove he didn't need any reminders today.

He raced over the remaining fences and, still pulling, galloped across the finish line. Katie dismounted and weighed in, breathlessly jubilant at his exhilarating clear round. When Alan hurried up to tell her she was lying second, Katie thought life was becoming almost unreal.

She led her wonderful Goose back to the stables and hosed down his cut shoulder, which happily had not bothered him at all. Soon Gossip was clean and dry and rugged up, tucking into his supper. Katie went to bed in a stupor; she could not believe her marvellous day.

Before the vets' inspection the next morning, Katie walked Gossip for an hour to ease any stiff muscles before he was trotted up. Then as she jogged him past the presiding ground jury, her high spirits dropped to the floor. Gossip was unlevel. He was feeling some soreness in his bruised left shoulder. Amazingly the ground jury were lenient. They asked Katie to walk him around for a further five minutes and then bring him back for re-examination. On his second trot up he was sound. Katie, overwhelmed with relief, burst into tears.

She was so rattled after the morning's dramas she forgot to walk the show-jumping course, set for that afternoon.

'Never mind,' muttered Katie, still feeling weak at the knees that they had so nearly missed this last phase altogether.

Gossip felt stiff and Katie cantered and worked him for half an hour before he jumped. He was less apprehensive in the ring but this time had one pole down, though it did not affect his placing. Katie was ecstatic. She had never dreamt of finishing so high up the order. One of the first people to congratulate her was Lucinda, whose mare, Hysterical, had fallen and been retired on the steeplechase.

Life was rather flat after the excitement of Tidworth. Gossip was turned out for his summer holiday and Katie continued her work at Ashbrooke.

Gossip's achievements, whilst acknowledged at the time, were still no 'big deal', as Katie put it, as far as his ascendancy up the eventing ladder was concerned. Ashbrooke was not a professional competition yard, so whatever the horses accomplished was incidental to the reasons Ashbrooke existed – though, of course, when they were successful, the horses helped keep the name in the public eye, which was good for business. The event horses' careers were plotted from season to season, rather than from year to year, depending on what riders were available at the time.

Gossip's career, and ultimately his future, might have taken a very different course had Katie not visited some friends for supper soon after her return from Tidworth.

'Did you realise, Katie, that Gossip has qualified for Burghley?' someone casually asked that evening.

Katie's jaw dropped open. 'You don't mean it, surely?' she gaped.

'Go and look up the rules,' another voice advised, 'I think you'll find he has.'

Katie couldn't wait to leave, and when she returned to Ashbrooke that night she dug out the rule book which laid out qualifications for championship three-day events. She discovered her friends were right.

What a chance for her and the Goose, bubbled Katie's thoughts. But how best to suggest the idea to the Brookes?

After all, Gossip was not Katie's horse. Katie was an employee of the Brookeboroughs and had duties and responsibilities at Ashbrooke. No other horses at Ashbrooke were being considered for Burghley so the finances for the trip could not be diluted as they had been for Tidworth. Problems could arise on the journey over; Gossip might become lame or sick in England before the event started, which would make the whole trip a very expensive waste of time.

These thoughts and a hundred other 'ifs' and possible snags buzzed around Katie's brain, as she tried to pluck up courage to ask Lady Brookeborough what she thought of the idea.

After a few days spent agonising, Katie remembered the well-known adage, 'Nothing ventured, nothing gained', and blurted out her discovery to Lady Brookeborough.

'What?' answered a surprised Lady Brookeborough, thinking she had not heard Katie correctly.

'Well, he seems to be qualified,' stammered Katie. 'And I'll pay for the entry fee.'

'Well,' came the reply from Lady Brookeborough, thinking hard, 'you can go ahead and enter him, but I cannot give you any guarantee you will be able to go,' which Katie well understood.

Gossip was duly entered and nothing more was said. Katie even feared, as July turned to August, that everyone had forgotten about Burghley as no one even hinted at the possibility of the trip.

Katie gave Gossip a shorter summer holiday this year as the Burghley dates were at the end of the second week of September. Throughout the summer Gossip was worked and schooled on the flat by Lady Brookeborough and Katie, and kept to a strict fitness schedule. In the background lay Burghley, an unconfirmed and indistinct goal.

Then one day in the latter half of August, Katie knew Burghley had not been forgotten. Over breakfast, Lord Brookeborough suddenly fired a question at her.

'Jumped many drops lately, Katie?'

'Er no, not really,' mumbled Katie, wondering what was coming. 'Well,' his Lordship announced, 'I'm going to build you one today.'

Borrowing the services of an estate worker, Lord Brookeborough disappeared into one of the fields at Ashbrooke where there was a very steep hill. They set about hammering in two solid stakes then tied a substantial pole at a fair height between them.

Katie brought Gossip out to the field, eyeing Lord Brookeborough's construction with apprehension.

'There you are, Katie.' Lord Brookeborough waved his arm airily, indicating the fence perched on the near-vertical slope. 'Just canter down the hill and pop over that.'

Katie gulped, picked up the reins and cantered down the hill. Gossip pinged neatly over the pole and skipped to the bottom of the slope.

'Oh, that's fine. Perfectly all right,' breezed his Lordship cheerfully, as he loped down the hill towards them. 'Burghley will be no problem!'

And that was the sum total of Gossip's cross-country schooling for Burghley.

Katie did manage to take Gossip to an open intermediate event on the last day of August, which he won and which boosted their confidence a little more assuredly towards the apparent level of Lord Brookeborough's.

Burghley was just around the corner. Katie gave Gossip his final gallop before they crossed the Irish Sea. Gossip gave Katie added reassurance when she felt for the first time he was happy and secure at this pace and was no longer trying to run away from himself. As Gossip contentedly jogged his way back across the fields to Ashbrooke, Katie could hardly believe it was only two years ago that she had volunteered to look after the then miserable bad-tempered gelding whom nobody wanted.

Katie and Ivan Fowler, who was to act as her groom for the competition, and who adored Gossip and was one of the few men Gossip trusted, set out with Gossip in a trailer for the sea-port of Larne. Lord and Lady Brookeborough were to follow later. They crossed by ferry to Stranraer in Scotland, and drove down through the night to Lincolnshire, reaching Burghley at nine o'clock the following morning.

The stately park evoked a dignified yet warm welcome. Katie unloaded Gossip off the trailer and installed him in his allotted temporary stable, which was one of many erected especially for the week of the trials. Gossip was unimpressed with his living quarters and within five minutes had smashed a hole in the wooden walls with a hind leg. Katie cursed for not sooner fastening one of his hobbles onto his off hind and went to summon a carpenter to repair the damage.

Apart from threatening to reduce his stable to matchwood, Gossip settled in well, unbothered by the ordered bustle of other horses and people coming and going all day long. He usually kept his bottom to the door, which detracted curious eyes as he appeared such an uninteresting horse.

During the two days before the dressage, Katie hacked Gossip out and made a point of riding him down both sets of roads and tracks, which was permissible, to familiarise him with the route and in the hopes of avoiding the possibility of him napping on cross-country day, on at least those phases.

The main arena where the dressage and show-jumping were to be held was far grander than anything Katie or Gossip had encountered. Echoing, temporary covered stands gaped on three sides of the arena, the fourth side being for those without seat tickets and offering a raised wooden platform, open to the elements. In the middle of the arena lay glistening white boards marking the dressage test boundaries. On top of the dressage letter markers sat pots of flowers. Katie wondered if Goose would walk past them without shying.

When Katie walked the steeplechase course, which encircled a golf course, she was pleased to see that the fences were less formidable than those of Tidworth, and that there was no hill down which she might suffer brake failure.

The cross-country course, as it so often does to many first-time competitors, looked perfectly feasible to Katie's eyes.

Burghley course designer, Bill Thompson, is a past master at devising deceptively modest-looking fences that do not *appear* to hold any unforeseen problems. But if his courses are not attacked with strong, precise riding they can catch out any rider, from the rawest newcomer to the most seasoned campaigner.

With the supreme confidence she had in Gossip, no course had ever looked frightening, but Katie knew she must not fall into the trap of underestimating one of the world's most famous event courses.

As well as the hacking, Gossip was undergoing his usual routine of lungeing and schooling. In the hours before the test Katie lunged Gossip for one and a half hours before riding him. She was becoming so nervous at the prospect of entering that smart arena that she could hardly keep herself from shaking. Lady Brookeborough, in sympathy, handed Katie a tot of whisky to calm her nerves, hoping that the benefits might spread to Gossip if Katie was more relaxed.

Unluckily, Gossip followed Gurgle the Greek, ridden by Rachel Bayliss, who always produced superlative tests and would therefore make Gossip's look all the worse in the judges' eyes. Rachel's performance at this Burghley was no exception. She left the arena to enthusiastic applause and went on to take the lead with a score of 38, which was unsurpassed over the two days of dressage.

The Brookes and Ivan held their breath as Gossip went into the arena, but he trotted in without any thoughts of napping. When the bell rang to signify the judges were ready, he cantered quietly up the centre line to halt at X while Katie bowed to them. 'Three judges,' thought Katie. 'How grand!'

To Katie's utter delight Gossip did relax, at least as much as she could hope for, and they left the arena in the sure knowledge that it was Gossip's best test ever.

'You gorgeous Goose,' Katie exclaimed, as she slithered off him once they were back in the collecting ring, and plied him with his favourite Fox's Glacier Mints. As a measure of Gossip's consistency, all three judges had awarded them an identical amount of good marks, giving Gossip a final total of 66 penalty points and placing them eighteenth.

Taut faces and strained smiles abounded in the stables on cross-country morning, as riders and grooms strove to keep nerves at bay. Horses peered expectantly over their doors, alert to the anticipation in the atmosphere that always prevails until the first competitor sets out on phase A and releases the tension with the sudden action.

As Katie was number 59 she had nearly three hours to while away, so she helped quell her nerves by walking parts of the course to study how the early competitors were faring, and to make a mental note of any problems.

Gossip was sensible at the start of phase A, and he and Katie arrived, without incident, on time at the beginning of phase B. Gossip hurtled round the steeplechase at his normal terrifying speed, and Katie did not dare check her time against her watch as to do so meant taking a hand off the reins, and that would have been akin to driving downhill with no brakes. Katie was sure Gossip would be unpenalised on time anyway, he was so fast, and she was right. They scooted through the finish and on to phase C, clear on both counts. Gossip was hopelessly unsettled on phase C as, knowing the route, he was aware the stables lay ahead of him. He refused to adopt any sort of rhythm and lurched and plunged between trot and canter the six-odd miles of roads and tracks back to the Box.

When Katie came through the finish of phase C, she almost fell off in the Box through total exhaustion. Gossip was dripping with sweat and the two pairs of reins were slippery with foam. Katie gasped, 'I'll never be able to hold him on the cross country,' and slumped down helplessly on to an upturned bucket, adding with a wail, 'and Goose must be shattered too, wasting all that energy on phase C.'

Gossip, looking far from tired as he tried to catch Ivan with one of his cow-kicks, was rapidly being washed down and his reins rubbed dry with a towel. Lady Brookeborough took charge. She told Katie to shut up and not be so silly, then handed her a drink. Not whisky this time, but water heavily laced with glucose. Katie gulped down the entire glassful and immediately doubled over with the most agonising stitch. Poor Katie staggered round the Box groaning, bending and straightening in an attempt to relieve what felt like a knife digging in her side. All too soon it was time to remount

Gossip. Lady Brookeborough skilfully legged her up, as usual from somewhere in the region of Gossip's head to avoid his heels.

Katie sat upright with a grimace of pain and picked up the reins.

'Well, good luck, Katie.' Lady Brookeborough forced through an optimistic smile. By this time the entire Brooke contingent's nerves were in tatters, knowing how weak Katie felt, and they were almost certain she hadn't a hope of completing on such a hard puller as Gossip. But, still, they felt duty-bound to try and boost the rider's dwindling strength and confidence.

Katie walked Gossip into the start box of phase D.

'Two . . . one . . . Go!' Nothing happened. Gossip stood rooted to the spot, head up, ears back and eyes rolling in their sockets. With his inherent instinct for bad timing he had napped.

Katie froze in the saddle, her mind in a whirl.

'They were all right,' she panicked, 'I'll never get him going,' remembering the advice and comments from Scarva. Then, in a flash, she remembered something else from Scarva. Without even picking up the reins, she commanded 'Canter on!' in a tone as close as she could muster to Lady Brookeborough's. Gossip unlocked his body, put his head down and cantered sedately out onto the course. It was hard to believe there was no lunge line attached.

Katie breathed again and scrabbled for the reins as Gossip accelerated, all attention now on the first fence.

He barely acknowledged the early fences, and after the third, headed in a right-handed loop across the park to the fourth, which was a yawning ditch with a stiff brush behind. As Gossip hurtled towards it, Katie could not steady his pace enough to direct him to where she wanted him to take off. Not helping matters was the fact that Gossip was conscious of the stables somewhere to his right, and he began to veer towards them. Katie could tell by his flicking ears that his concentration was not on the fence, now only strides in front of them. Katie pulled with all her strength on the left rein. Gossip took off, still with his mind on the stables, and sailed over the extreme right-hand side of the fence. Katie is convinced to this day that Gossip was not aware of what he was doing.

Thankfully, they landed safely and careered down to the next fence, the double coffin. All Katie could think of as she battled grimly against their headlong rush was, 'And I've come to England for this?' Gossip pulled relentlessly at Katie's jellified arm muscles, her strength all gone like water down a plug-hole. Katie leant back against the reins, using her weight in a vain hope that it might slow up his headlong flight to the coffin. Gossip still hadn't forgotten about the stables, and each stride took him another foot to the right. Katie anchored her hand onto the left rein, and Gossip flipped through the coffin elements like they were cavaletti, concentration a million miles away.

After the double coffin the course swung sharply left, away from the stables, and the sixth fence was lapped rails into a wood. For the first time Katie actually had to use her legs when Gossip briefly checked himself as he jumped from light into dark, combined with the realisation that 'home' was now behind him. Fence seven in the wood was a trappy rail in a ditch. For a moment Katie moved her hand off the rein, thinking she might need her stick as Gossip sized up the situation. With a flurry of hooves Gossip fiddled his way across, needing no encouragement from Katie, and blasted his way out of the wood towards the Irish Bank. At this fence Lady Brookeborough had given Katie strict instructions on their course walk: 'Katie, you must make a definite leap onto the bank, one stride and leap off again.'

Gossip galloped towards the mound. Katie, so relieved they had made it this far unscathed, forgot all orders and allowed him to hop up, shuffle across the top and plop down the other side.

As Gossip landed off the bank, Katie remembered her instructions, and thought 'Oh dear, I'm going to be in trouble for this.' And a second later she smiled to herself. 'But I don't care!' Katie suddenly realised she was having the ride of her life.

The Trout Hatchery which followed, Gossip made look easy. He had always loved jumping into water, which never held any fears for him. An uphill gallop brought them to the straightforward water-trough fence, and then an inviting, but wide brush fence, that the Brookes thought Gossip might bank, but he flew over without touching so much as a twig.

Katie took a check, which thankfully Gossip answered, at Capability's Cutting. It comprised a set of rails on the lip of a near-vertical slope which dropped into the 'Cutting'. Then the horses had to generate a lot of impulsion to propel themselves up the face of the opposite bank and over a further set of rails. Once again, Lucinda, who was without a ride at Burghley, had offered Katie some advice beforehand: 'Hook right back, Katie, as you come in, then at the bottom of the cutting thump him with your legs.'

Katie hooked and Gossip went. No thumps were needed. The following fence, the zig-zag wall, produced an oath from Lady Brookeborough, who was watching on the close-circuit TV in the Box, as Katie took a different route from the one they had originally planned. But it came off, and they galloped quickly away towards the second half of the course.

Gossip was utterly brilliant. He operated like a smoothly oiled machine on the second half. Not one fence did he meet wrong or think twice about. Between his fences he galloped fast and absolutely on line for the next obstacle. Katie talked to him all the way, unable to believe the thrilling ride she was having. For the first time Katie felt Gossip really looked at what he was jumping, as he set himself up properly before each fence, rather than just skittering over it. It had needed a course such as Burghley to make Gossip think. In the past he had seemed to clear obstacles merely because they were in his way.

At the second-last, Katie asked Gossip to shorten his stride for take-off. Gossip's reply to that was, 'Leave it to me.' He took off early and put in a huge leap. A hundred yards further on Gossip soared over the last and sprinted for the finish, still with energy to spare.

Minutes later, the loudspeaker announced that Gossip had moved into the lead. Although Katie knew he wouldn't stay in that position for long, as there were still several very good horses and riders to go, it was perfectly wonderful to revel in the euphoria of temporarily lying first. What a horse, and only fifteen minutes earlier Katie had thought she was too weak to even sit on him. Feeling ten feet tall, Katie joined the rejoicing Brookes and Ivan, and they all took a steaming but contented Gossip back to the stables.

By the end of the day Gossip had dropped only two places. The dressage leader, Rachel, had run into trouble and fallen out of the reckoning. Aly Pattinson on Carawich had taken over the lead from Richard Meade, lying second on Tommy Buck.

At 7 am on Sunday morning Katie checked Gossip over to see that no bumps or bruises had developed overnight. Ivan lunged him for threequarters of an hour before the vets' inspection, to loosen and warm up Gossip's muscles. This time he passed without any problem.

At Burghley Katie made sure she remembered to walk the show-jumping course, but wasn't able to glean much advice from her companion, younger sister Caroline, who accompanied her but who had never been to an event before.

The Brookeboroughs were already trying to calm their nerves at the bar in the members' tent. Lord Brookeborough did accompany Katie on a second walk, but neither of them felt there were any major problems.

In the parade of competitors that preceded the show-jumping, Gossip was the model of decorum and walked the entire way round the circumference of the arena.

As the show-jumping began, Katie watched the first few competitors. This phase ran in reverse order of merit, so Katie was third last to jump. As his time drew nearer, Katie mounted Gossip and rode him over to the practice jumps to work him under the eye of Lady Brookeborough. Gossip was jumping well and picked his feet up carefully over the practice fences.

'Now number 59, Village Gossip, owned by the Viscount and Viscountess Brookeborough, and ridden by Katie O'Hara,' blared the loudspeaker across the arena and packed stands.

Ivan had to lead Gossip in as Katie could feel he was thinking of napping. She trotted over to the VIPs' box and saluted the Marquis of Exeter, owner of Burghley House. As she bowed her head Katie thought, 'This is crazy. Here I am, saluting in front of all these people.' Katie grinned as she stared up at Lord Exeter. She felt sure she would wake up in a minute from what was seeming more and more like a fantastic dream, or else a huge joke! In Katie's mind, it was the cross-country day that had been really important to her. Its outcome had been so incredibly marvellous that anything good that happened after it could only count as a bonus. If she messed up the show-juming, she honestly didn't mind.

The bell ringing to start her round jolted Katie out of her day-dream, and she closed her legs on Gossip's sides. She glanced at the collecting ring as Gossip moved into a canter. The Brookes lining the rails looked a collective bundle of nerves. From the almost green pallor of Lord Brookeborough's face, Katie wondered if he was going to be ill.

Gossip crossed the start and bounded over the first two fences. Katie happily thought, 'This is fine . . . so far.'

Halfway round, Katie loosed Gossip off at the water jump, which he cleared easily. But she then checked him back so sharply for the following fence, that Gossip had to more or less climb over to negotiate it, but the rails stayed in place. At the next fence, a spread close to the collecting ring, Katie applied her legs strongly, as it was perfectly sited for Gossip to have an excuse to nap. He sailed over without hesitation and faced up to the last combination, still clear. As she lined Gossip up, Katie thought 'I've done it,' followed instantaneously by the premonition, 'No, I haven't.' Her concentration had lapsed in those vital seconds and Gossip was all wrong for the first part. He skewed over and knocked it down, and Katie couldn't think how they were going to make the second element. Gossip's agility coped with that problem but another pole hit the ground. Miraculously he cleared the third part and left it intact. Gossip had dropped to eighth.

As Katie and Gossip left the arena to sympathetic applause, someone said to Katie, 'God just wasn't on your side today, was he?' to which Katie replied with a broad smile, 'Oh but he was. It was Him who got me here in the first place.'

Back at Ashbrooke, Katie was worried. Gossip's performance

at Burghley had earned him recognition and other people in the event world had begun to take an interest in him. He was now worth a lot of money. There was every possibility he would be sold. Katie miserably contemplated her future. Life at Ashbrooke just would not be the same without her Goose.

It wasn't long before Katie's fears were realised. There was a definite buyer. It was Lucinda. Katie's mind flashed back to what she now saw was more than just casual interest on the Prior-Palmers' part, when they watched Gossip at Tidworth, or even when they had seen him in the school way back in January. Katie suddenly remembered how she had noticed Lucinda and top trainer, Dick Stillwell, observing Gossip intently and conferring, a few feet away, as she unsaddled him at the end of the cross country at Burghley. She had thought little of it at the time.

By mid-December the deal was clinched. Gossip's new rider was to be the new European Champion, crowned only that September on her star of Badminton, Be Fair.

Not being able to face seeing Gossip go, Katie left Ashbrooke before he did. When she went to say goodbye to Gossip, she left a packet of his favourite mints with the person who was to look after him until Gossip left for England, with instructions to give him one or two a day.

A month after Gossip had gone, Katie returned to Ashbrooke on a visit. In his stable she found, tucked behind the window grille, a dusty packet of unopened mints.

4 Two Steps Forward, One Step Back

Lucinda's first proper recollection of Gossip was at his second Tidworth in 1975, and her initial impressions were similar in a way to those of Lady Brookeborough's, 'Nice little horse', but no more than that. Her next and most vivid memories were at Burghley that same year, where Gossip made her really sit up and take notice. His style of jumping was almost unbelievable – he decelerated from 30mph to 5mph amidst a flurry of dust, squirmed over the fence, and within two strides was off at the same incredible rate. That he pulled was obvious, and Lucinda remembers Katie leaning back as she approached each fence in a vain effort to slow him up. Because of his speed and attacking style Lucinda quickly appreciated his phenomenal athleticism. She also understood that he and Katie had formed a tightly bonded partnership, though discipline was not part of it. Gossip's round at Burghley, was, to Lucinda's eyes, the most scintillating and exciting of the day.

But Lucinda did not want Gossip. In her stables that autumn stood two outstanding advanced eventers, her own Be Fair and Mrs Vicky Phillips' Wideawake. To obtain another would have made her look nothing other than avaricious. But Lady Doreen, Lucinda's mother, did not agree and was looking farther ahead to the future. Wideawake had produced tendon trouble the previous year, and although was now sound, the problem could flare up again. Which left Be Fair, who was twelve and would not last for ever. Lucinda saw her mother's wisdom and acquiesced to the decision to try and buy Gossip.

The Prior-Palmers' first major hurdle was to find a

benefactor who would put up the money to buy Gossip. As the search for a sponsor dragged into the winter, Lucinda, after a triumphant victory on Wideawake at the Dutch three-day-event championships at Boekelo, set out on her pre-arranged trip to Iran, where she was to spend two months teaching. She still had no idea if she would be able to have Gossip and up to then had not even sat on him. This may seem the height of flippancy but the Prior-Palmers knew the Brookeboroughs well, had followed Gossip's progress closely, and Lucinda was undoubtedly more experienced than Katie. It never dawned on them that Gossip would be anything other than 'all right'.

Eventually, Bob Dean of British Equestrian Promotions put the Prior Palmers in touch with businessman David Kingsley, who subsequently became Gossip's new owner.

'Legs of iron; marvellous stamp of horse,' enthused Major-General Prior-Palmer, Lucinda's father, who was normally referred to as 'the General'. 'But he does kick a bit,' continued the General. 'Has to wear hobbles in the stable,' he added, as though the matter was of minor importance.

I was less certain. I had looked after Lucinda's horses for two years and had recently learnt that Gossip was to join us. I had, in fact, been briefly introduced to Gossip in 1974, when the Brookeboroughs and Katie had stayed at Appleshaw for a night after Tidworth. Gossip had glared suspiciously at me as I poked my head over the door, and he waved a hind leg as Katie, unperturbed, carried on straightening his rugs.

The next morning I watched in fascinated awe as Katie groomed him. Heels flew as Gossip tried to stop the brush tickling his body, and then, as Katie laughingly ignored him, he all but fell on top of her when she groomed his tummy. I couldn't imagine how she managed to put a tail bandage on him. As Katie worked round him Gossip rocked his weight from hind foot to hind foot, ready to let fly at any moment. Katie seemed oblivious to the imminent danger and chatted to him as though he was a small child. I had no idea of the intense rapport between them and thought Katie extraordinarily brave. I was fervently glad that I had nothing to do with him.

Now here I was, eighteen months later, faced with having to look after the same horse I had viewed from the safety of the other side of the door, without any idea of how to go about it.

Naturally Gossip was carefully vetted prior to purchase, and at last the matter of his heart problem was cleared up.

After Richard Coghlan had declined to buy him, the Brookeboroughs were initially extremely worried that Gossip's heart was not as it should be. However, their fears diminished over the next two years as Gossip took on more strenuous work, and indeed needed so much work, without any signs of stress or strain. He never gave them any cause for alarm when Katie evented, and it was concluded that there could not have been too much wrong in the first place.

The Prior-Palmers sent over Peter Scott-Dunn, official vet to the British Team, to examine Gossip. Peter discovered that Gossip's heart missed one beat in four when at rest. When Gossip was worked his heart picked up to the normal rate. An hour or so after work, if Gossip was just standing quietly in his stable, his heart dropped back to missing a beat. Peter did not feel this was reason enough to fail him, but he advised a second opinion from a heart specialist. The specialist confirmed all Peter's findings and conclusions, and went on to add that it even indicated a stronger heart because Gossip's did less work than normal hearts at rest. As long as the heart kept to regular beats when Gossip worked there would be no problem.

Lucinda returned from Iran in the New Year, and almost immediately left again for Northern Ireland with her little cream-coloured horsebox. She was intending to spend a week at Ashbrooke to acquaint herself with Gossip, whilst Lady Brookeborough, who knew him as well as Katie, was on hand to offer advice. Through her parents, who had been to see Gossip that winter, Lucinda was beginning to understand that Gossip's temperament was a little more complex than merely that of a sensitive thoroughbred. She even asked me if I would like to have him ready clipped out for the spring season before he left Ireland, realising that he could be difficult, and it would be one less hassle to have to cope with until we knew him better. I firmly agreed.

The day after she arrived at Ashbrooke, Lucinda rode

Gossip in the indoor school and was slightly surprised to find that Gossip flatly refused to come onto the bit, which was rather unusual for an advanced event horse.

'Oh, well,' thought Lucinda, and shrugged it off. She found it difficult to put any horse on the bit. She presumed that eventually she and Gossip would come to the sort of compromise that she had arrived at with Be Fair and Wideawake, and the problem would sort itself out. That compromise was not reached for another five years.

The second morning Lucinda took Gossip for a hack. En route she jumped him over a couple of small cross-country fences. Or rather, Gossip took charge and hurtled over them in his usual haste. Lucinda, whilst revelling in his fantastic jump, was a little concerned that she could do nothing to slow him down and that it was going to take nerves of iron to gallop into fixed fences at such a terrifying speed.

Lucinda returned to the yard at Ashbrooke a little red in the face from her exertions, and said to Lady Brookeborough, 'Well, he's marvellous . . . er . . did he always pull so hard with Katie? He is a bit strong.' Lady Brookeborough, so used to Gossip's way across country, couldn't think what Lucinda was fussing about. After all, Katie hadn't been too bothered and had survived unscathed. She dismissed Lucinda's qualms by telling her he was always a bit strong and that there was nothing to worry about. Lucinda accepted her reassurances, thinking anyway that it was probably her 'electric' bottom that had caused Gossip to tear off at such a rate.

On January 27th, Emma Murdoch, Appleshaw's first working pupil, and I watched apprehensively as the horsebox trundled up the drive. Ominous rattling thumps resounded from the interior as Gossip protested against his hobbles, the chains of which were clipped together as there were no rings on the floor of the horsebox to attach them to. Lucinda slowed to a halt, jumped out of the cab, and walked round to drop the side-ramp. Lurking behind a half-eaten haynet was a dark brown face, split by a thin white stripe. Gossip peered out, darting a quick glance at his new home. Then he noticed Emma and me looking at him. His ears flattened and he snapped his teeth, pulling his head back inside the safety of the horsebox. Lesson number one: Gossip hates being stared at, I thought.

Gossip did not want to know us. In the months that followed, I came to think that this could not possibly be the same horse that Katie had known and loved at Ashbrooke. Lady Brookeborough had told Lucinda of Gossip's extreme mistrust of everyone and everything when he had arrived at Ashbrooke, until Katie began to look after him. And then how slowly and carefully they had built up his confidence, and how his character had altered. Lucinda passed on this knowledge to Emma and me, and so, knowing something of what Gossip had been through, we were prepared to be very sympathetic towards him and encourage him to be friends. Gossip had other ideas. As far as he was concerned we were all under the gravest suspicion for an indefinite period, with absolutely no guarantee of acceptance at the end.

For most of that spring, Gossip reverted to his old aggressive habits, hiding his sorrow at losing Katie and at finding himself in an unfamiliar place, behind a façade of fierce indifference. He could sense that the strangers now surrounding him were well-meaning and unlikely to harm him or treat him roughly, but he was also intensely aware of our caution and that we did not completely trust him not to kick or bite us.

To begin with, neither Emma nor I could even put a headcollar on him in the stable. For the first week he was at Appleshaw, he was looked after almost entirely by Lucinda, with whom he was a little more familiar and who was much braver than Emma or me. In turn, we steeled ourselves to ignore his threatening heels and his bottom stationed by the door, as we edged into his stable with a feed or a haynet, or to muck him out.

Gossip was kept in both hobbles, unjoined, on his back legs, for the simple reason that he could not move around the stable so quickly and was therefore easier to catch. He frequently made me look an utter idiot on occasions when Lucinda asked for him to be tacked up. She would return ten minutes later only to find me still being whirled round the stable, hanging on to the front of his rugs.

This was not a method of catching I wanted to adopt permanently as it did little to encourage Gossip's trust in us. It threw him into a panic, wondering what was going to happen, and it tested our nerves because he spun at an alarming rate, and it was quite a feat to hang on until he decided to stop. Then, when he did stop, there was the tricky business of putting on the headcollar before he took fright and started spinning again. The key was to show complete trust in him, even if you didn't always feel it.

We invented another method. I would approach his rear end, backwards – this was the only part of Gossip that faced us whenever we entered his stable. Still facing backwards, I would bend down and pretend to examine a hind leg. Staying bent, I would shuffle backwards and run a hand down a front leg. Gossip would keep a wary eye on me throughout, but this slow oblique approach did not seem to fill him with so much suspicion as a direct attack. All the while I would amuse him with a spate of inane chatter. Then came the difficult part as I would attempt to straighten up and, still facing the tail, quietly slide a rope under his neck and drop the end over his crest. If I showed any sign of hurrying or impatience he would move away, his intuition so acutely sensitive. Then I would have to begin with the hind leg all over again. Once I had the rope round his neck, he would allow the headcollar to be buckled on and was easy enough to tack up.

This new idea was a great step forward in opening the communication line between ourselves and Gossip. We also *did* begin to trust him. On several occasions Emma and I found ourselves in situations where Gossip, if he had wanted to, could have thwacked us with a hind leg, especially when we utilised our new method of catching him. But he never did harm us, and so we began to break through his barrier of self-imposed aggression and dilute the ferocious exterior he portrayed. As the weeks progressed he became more relaxed in our company, and a day of great achievement came when we were able to put a headcollar on in his stable without the preliminary overtures.

But our problems were not over once we had mastered the catching problem. Gossip tried our patience in many other ways. Whatever took twenty minutes to accomplish with any other horse often took twice as long with Gossip.

He was extremely ticklish to groom, as I had witnessed when watching Katie two years earlier. He kicked and fidgeted as I wielded the brush, even if the bristles were the softest I could find. When it was feasible I washed the most ticklish parts, such as his sheath area and between and behind his front legs, thinking it kinder to both of us if I removed the dried sweat this way, rather than battling away for hours with a brush. It was unfortunate that Gossip, being so hot-blooded, sweated profusely when he worked.

Simple tasks like pulling his mane and tail, caused havoc. He didn't mind his mane being done, so long as I only picked at it with my fingers. If I used a mane comb, he would pin me against the wall, then toss and shake his head so I could neither move, nor catch hold of his mane. As for his tail, I bow in deference to Katie's skill and incredible rapport with him. How she succeeded in accomplishing the deed is a mystery. Even with the hobbles clipped together, Gossip bucked and slammed his backside into me as I carefully whisked out a hair or two at a time. Although I did not want to, I had to resort to using a twitch, which did at least stop him bucking. His tail eventually looked roughly the correct shape, but it was never as smart as Katie's professional finish. Someone once suggested I let Gossip's tail grow out, but he would never have permitted anyone to plait it for competitions.

Putting on a tail bandage was a trial, especially if you valued your knee-caps. If I inadvertently caught a hair or pulled one while winding on the bandage, Gossip would tap me smartly on the knee with a hind hoof as though to say, 'Watch it!'

His tail never looked very good, as, apart from my pathetic efforts at pulling it, the bottom half was very thin, a permanent reminder of the donkey's attacks when Gossip was a yearling. In summer it became even thinner, as Gossip constantly swished it at the flies.

He behaved like a wriggling eel when being rugged up. He shifted his weight from side to side as each blanket was piled on, so by the time they were all in place, some hung more to the right, others to the left.

Gossip always cow-kicked from habit whenever the roller or girth was done up. I soon became wise to this but had to stand by his shoulder to be out of range. I found there was a rhythm to his swipes and it became quite easy to work between them.

All the horses at Appleshaw were given an hour or so in the field each day to relax and enjoy a change of scene, as well as gain from the obvious feeding benefits. Lucinda didn't want Gossip to be any different. It was with some trepidation that I let Gossip loose in the back field, albeit with a headcollar left on. I wondered if there was anyone in the neighbourhood who knew how to use a lassoo. We turned Gossip out an hour before lunch in the hopes he would be hungry and want to come in, as the grazing at that time of year was rather poor. The idea worked, and Gossip readily came up to us as we proffered a bribe of a scoop of nuts.

He did not always behave so amiably and many times it needed three people to corner him in the field. Gossip would then turn his elusiveness into a game and make sure we all had a fair amount of exercise before we finally channelled him into a corner. Even then he still did not give in, but would rear up waving his front feet at us in a mock attack. So we just had to wait until he became bored and let us walk forward and clip a rope onto his headcollar.

If we had not been able to fall back on the hobbles in those initial months, I think Gossip would have been practically impossible to look after. They slowed up his movement in the stable and thus diminished the power of his kick, which allowed us a less hazardous route to seek his trust. Until I knew him better I even connected them when I groomed him. And they were always put on when he travelled in the horsebox. They were also the cause of a funny incident.

Brough Scott, noted racing commentator and freelance journalist, arrived in the yard one morning to interview Lucinda. He was chatting to Emma as Lucinda drove up the driveway in the horsebox, having just worked Gossip on the hills, which were too far away to hack to. 'Sorry I'm late,' said Lucinda, as she ran round to the side-ramp and led Gossip out.

'Er, Lucinda,' babbled Emma, pointing at Gossip, then

dissolving into giggles. Lucinda glanced up as she urged Gossip, who was being awfully slow, down the ramp. Then she saw Brough staring open-mouthed at Gossip. She turned around. Gossip was shuffling behind her like an old man. Lucinda had forgotten to remove the connected hobbles from his back legs. With an embarrassed giggle Lucinda bent down and removed them and Emma led a pained Gossip back to his stable, for he realised the laughter was directed at him.

While Emma and I made some headway in the stable with Gossip, he was nothing like as co-operative under the saddle. Dressage meant submission, and submission was not in Gossip's vocabulary. Long arguments ensued whenever he was schooled. He adamantly refused to relax and soften the under-muscle on his neck. Whatever movements Lucinda tried, nothing induced him to come onto the bit.

Lucinda resorted to lungeing, and one day sent me out to a corner of the field (we had no enclosed school then) with Gossip in tow, to try and obtain some sort of a correct outline. I adjusted the side-reins so they were comfortable, but not too slack, stood in the centre of the circle and asked Gossip to walk on. He obliged for about three steps. Then he trotted. Then he cantered. The canter became a rabbity scuttle as Gossip leaned in at a forty-five-degree angle, like a motor-bike. I might as well have been giving the commands in Chinese for all the effect my voice had on Gossip. Clearly I didn't have the Brookeborough tone. I forced him to a halt by heading him into an overgrown thorn hedge which he skidded into, the prickles brushing his nose. I tried him on the other rein. This time Gossip behaved beautifully on the sides where he was penned in by the fence, but every third circuit, he stopped dead halfway round the open side of the circle, and waltzed backwards across the field, a crafty smirk spreading over his features. It felt like playing a benevolent shark on the end of a fishing line, but that shark was far smarter than the fisherman.

As Gossip became more at home at Appleshaw, it became rapidly apparent that his aggression was transforming itself into the most evil sense of humour, of which I had become one of his first victims. We had to think five minutes ahead of

Gossip to try and anticipate what mischief he was next going to plot, but all too often his quick-thinking caught us out.

It also did not take us long to discover his hatred of plastic bags. At first he merely shied at them when he passed them on the road. Then he developed the evasion into an excuse to nap, and would whip round on his hind legs each time he spied a bag. The only way he would then condescend to pass it was backwards.

We began to avoid riding him on the roads on rubbish-collection days, when the roads were lined with piles of brimming black polythene sacks awaiting the dust-cart. He wasn't so badly behaved if we led him off another horse. Then he just cannoned into whoever was leading him in an effort to keep as far away from the horror as possible. Like Katie we tried to cure him of his dislike, by placing a bag on the gravel outside his door. After twenty-four hours of listening to Gossip drumming his hind feet against the wall in fury we also had to admit defeat.

Our lungeing sessions did improve but they did not really help his dressage, apart from de-fizzing him a little. With a rider in the saddle, Gossip was tense and ungiving in his body, and the more the discipline was enforced, the worse he became. He had such stamina, both mental and physical, that it was impossible to tire him into submission. Certainly he tired to an extent, and then he became bad-tempered, not wishing to admit to the fact. When this happened he was horrid in the stable, so he was given only a cursory groom on those days then left to recover his humour in peace.

It was Lucinda's intention that year to ride Gossip at Badminton, as well as Wakey, her other entry. Be Fair had been excused competing as he was already on the short-list for the Olympics in Montreal and had proved himself a reliable cross-country horse over the years.

By the end of February, Lucinda was entertaining serious doubts about taking Gossip to Badminton. His dressage was an unfathomable mystery that eluded any offer of a compromise. In his canter (fitness) work he was impossible to hold and fought every step of the way. Consequently he split the corners of his lips and made his mouth sore. This meant that whenever Gossip was hacked out on the roads he was ridden in a headcollar with reins and draw-reins attached, as the less time a bit was in his mouth, the quicker the splits would heal. With Gossip being so uncontrollable, it seemed suicidal for Lucinda to tackle the Badminton fences without being able to dictate the speed.

At the end of the month, Gossip made his first public appearance with Lucinda, at a hunter trial near Bicester. Ditto, a five-year-old, was also to make his debut in the novice class. I was delegated to drive the two horses to Shelswell Park, whilst Lucinda, having a prior engagement, was to meet me there in her car.

Half an hour into the journey, I wondered if she was going to have any horses to ride at all. The noise in the back of the horsebox had escalated from an occasional thump to a full-scale battle. I pulled over and investigated. Gossip, who was never very amicable to his fellow equines, must have felt deeply insulted at having to travel with such a juvenile companion. Poor Ditto was enduring the most ferocious glowers and snapping of teeth. Gossip's hobbles rattled and crashed as he tried to kick out. In genuine terror, Ditto was panicking and thrashing his hooves in every direction in a futile attempt to escape from the monster beside him. The only solution I saw, was to tie them both up so short that they could do little more than blink. Gossip still succeeded in airing his feelings by rolling his eyeballs and rattling his hobbles threateningly for the rest of the journey.

Fortunately Ditto recovered his shattered nerves and cantered neatly round the novice course to record his first clear round. In the afternoon, it was Gossip's turn. Lucinda, not possessing a gag, decided to ride him in a double bridle, hoping that the curb rein would be strong enough to act as an emergency handbrake.

Gossip set off fighting hard against Lucinda, who was determined to control the pace and not let him have his own way. All went reasonably well until they came to a corner fence, under some trees. Gossip took off but drifted right, caught the fence with a leg and the impact shot Lucinda out of the saddle onto the ground. All I could think of as I watched them from two fields distant, was, 'Oh, do please hang onto the reins, Lucinda,' knowing I'd never catch him in the sprawling acres of parkland. Thankfully Lucinda did hang on, and hastily remounted to finish the course.

I was then presented with this steaming, sweating, fidgeting animal that seemed to have grown several extra legs that were all kicking at once. The General picked up and took a firm hold of a front leg whilst I brandished sponges, wishing I had telescopic arms. Gossip could still kick, despite standing on three legs, and the force when he did, jolted the sponge out of my hand. Lucinda, who was holding him, was being dragged backwards as Gossip pivoted away from my reach. By the time I had finished, I didn't know who was wetter, Gossip or us.

A week after the hunter trial, Lord and Lady Brookeborough happened to be in London on business. Lady Brookeborough volunteered to spend the weekend at Appleshaw to see if she could unknot some of the problems Lucinda was having.

On Saturday, armed with an assortment of bits and gadgets, they took Gossip up the circular tan gallop belonging to local racehorse trainer Toby Balding. As Lucinda lapped the circuits of the tan, using a different bit each time, Gossip became more aggressive and stronger as he raced away from the fight.

The more severe the bit, the more panicky he became and the harder he pulled. Lucinda gave up. She could see no alternative, other than sheer strength and a snaffle combined with a running martingale. A borrowed gag had not proved effective, and Lucinda hated riding cross country with two reins. His mouth was a real worry as every time he pulled, the corners split. The use of draw-reins when he cantered did help if used tactfully, but there seemed no answer to controlling him across country.

Gossip came back from the tan in one of his blackest moods. He was covered in tacky sweat, and the weather was too cold to give him a bath. I spent two hours scratching and brushing at his coat and he became crosser and crosser. He spent the remainder of the day skulking in the back of his box, bottom towards the door. When Emma or I entered with feed or hay, he snaked his head and neck round, ears back and teeth gnashing, as he waved a hind leg threateningly at us for daring to disturb his peace. He hated being messed about, and that was exactly how he considered his morning on the tan had been spent.

The weekend had brought no magical solutions, except a firm decision not to take Gossip to Badminton whilst they were so at odds with each other. Lucinda even abandoned taking him to his first intended event, Crookham, until a better understanding could be wrought between them.

At the end of March, Gossip went to Rushall one-day event, which, being a local event and attracting a large entry, meant he had to do his dressage the day before the event proper. He pranced his way through the test and that evening had a hot, swollen hind joint. A sprain was diagnosed and Gossip was withdrawn from the competition.

For the following two weeks Gossip was rested in the field, which fitted in well as Badminton week loomed nearer and Lucinda would not be there to ride him anyway. It also relieved Emma from the worry of having to hack him out whilst I was at Badminton looking after Wakey.

Wakey was not dissimilar to Gossip in that he was very sensitive to atmosphere and to the moods of humans. But in character he was different, very much the bumptious schoolboy. He had no manners and was always having to be led in a bridle and lunge rein as he was so strong and frequently escaped the clutches of his handlers. Loading him up for an event one day, Wakey towed me in, then straight out of the horsebox. Before I could tie him up, he pulled the rope out of my hands and shot up the alley-way, past the feed-shed and popped over the rails into the field. I hurried after in pursuit and found him about to sit down in a large patch of mud, wearing his best rug.

However, since winning Boekelo the previous autumn he had 'grown-up', and he sensed people no longer regarded him with exasperation. It had taken two years for Lucinda to 'click' with him, as he needed far more tactful riding than Be Fair. Wakey was brilliant and bold, but he was also reckless and would hurl himself over fences without really thinking. But now he was more mature and was in peak form to attack Badminton.

Lying fifth after the dressage, Wakey produced his brilliant best on the cross country to take the lead on the second day. On Sunday he show-jumped clear, something he rarely could be bothered to do, but this day he was a changed horse.

He won the Whitbread Trophy, fulfilling his owner's long-awaited dream, before fatally collapsing during his lap of honour, after the prize-giving.

Wakey was, as ever, tragically unique and individual to the end.

As Katie's intervention had reformed Gossip at Ashbrooke, so did Wakey's death, to a lesser extent, transform Gossip at Appleshaw.

Part of Gossip's antagonism at Appleshaw, we thought, was due to being relegated from number one horse in Ireland to number three at Appleshaw, behind Be Fair and Wakey. Suddenly he was no longer 'special' with a doting Katie behind him. Instead he was just one of several, and he had to watch Be Fair being indulged in the star treatment that he had been so recently enjoying at Ashbrooke.

Then, after Badminton, Gossip was moved into Wakey's stable. With that uncanny sense horses possess, Gossip knew something had happened. He was aware of the aura of sadness that pervaded the yard. In deference to the mood, Gossip mellowed and opened his affections to us. Somehow he knew he was now more important, and that extra responsibility had shifted to his shoulders now that he was understudy to Be Fair. So dramatic was this change we discarded his hobbles, using them only for travelling purposes.

At last Gossip showed his face to the eventing world with his new rider, at Henstridge in the open intermediate class. As he had fought with Ditto, he also tried to attack Lucinda's other ride in the intermediate, Hysterical, a brown mare owned by Mrs Joan Ivory. Hysterical was so named because of her batty temperament, and this time the fighting was so bad I could feel the horsebox swaying. I tied their noses to the wall and comparative peace reigned.

Henstridge was not an unduly difficult event. Gossip whizzed round the cross country just within the realms of safety, and Hysterical stayed sober and came second in her section.

A week later at Batsford, Gossip and Hysterical both finished third in their respective advanced and intermediate classes.

Then, for the third successive year, Gossip appeared at Tidworth three-day event. Lucinda felt the not over-taxing demands of the course would give her a chance to find out a little more about Gossip.

Although we were spared the exciting dramas the Brookes had suffered, I did nearly lose Gossip at the first vets' inspection.

I was leading him back to the horsebox park after he had been passed at the vetting. Gossip was very wound up and pulled and jogged beside me. I had almost reached the gate to cross the road when I heard a shout of 'Loose horse!' Glancing over my left shoulder, I saw a large bay gelding galloping straight towards us, rugs flapping and lead rein slapping against his legs. It was Hugh Thomas's Campanario, and Margaret, his groom, was in hot pursuit. Gossip and I were five yards from the fence, and a pile-up looked inevitable. I threw my weight back against Gossip's lead rein to halt him. With a swoosh, Campanario galloped past, between us and the fence, almost taking Gossip's nose off. I waited for Gossip to wrench the rein from my hands and gallop off, which is exactly what Wakey would have done. Amazingly, he didn't. He was so surprised, he trotted round me, snorting in astonishment.

Lucinda was also riding Hysterical at Tidworth. Once again the mare lived up to her name in the dressage and was bottom in her section. Gossip was not much better, though his movements did resemble a dressage test and his efforts were accorded a higher mark.

On cross-country day, I greased Gossip's legs before he even started phase A. None of us knew what his behaviour would be like in the Box prior to phase D, when the grease is normally applied, but, judging from one-day events, we anticipated him being fairly impossible. As it turned out, he was considerably easier than Wakey had ever been.

Gossip was horribly strong on the roads and tracks, never settling and expending needless energy as he bounced and bobbed his way to the steeplechase and then down phase C. On the steeplechase he was very fast, but mishap free. In the Box he behaved surprisingly well, except for the lethal cow-kicks which he fired at a rate of about one a second. Like the Brookes, I had to leg Lucinda up from somewhere near his head.

As had happened to Katie, Lucinda found she had very little control on the cross country. But Gossip's fantastic jump thrilled her in a way none of her horses had ever done before.

The following afternoon he went clear in the show-jumping to finish the competition third, once again his speed helping to overhaul other rivals with better dressage marks. Hysterical, too, had overcome her enormous dressage handicap and had leapt into tenth place.

After Tidworth, Gossip and Hysterical went out for a month's holiday and the two became firm friends, which was somewhat surprising since they never enjoyed each other's company when competing or travelling.

On Midsummer's Day Gossip started work in preparation for the autumn season. He had blossomed on his holiday, with no humans to pester him, and was contented and relaxed when he came in, beginning to accept that Appleshaw was now home.

One of his first outings was to accompany Be Fair for the final week of team training at Ribbesdale Park, Ascot, before the team flew out to Canada for the Olympic Games. The team riders were each allowed to take an extra horse to the training week – 'To keep them out of mischief,' Col. Bill Lithgow, then chef d'équipe of the team, once suggested with a chuckle.

Gossip, recognising the presence of those greater than himself, kept a humble profile. I felt so sorry for him being part of the chorus rather than a star, that I made quite a fuss of him. This infuriated Be Fair, who thought he was the only one entitled to VIP treatment.

At the end of the week Gossip returned to Appleshaw, to be looked after by Tracy Sohn, who had replaced Emma as working pupil. Whilst we were in Canada, Tracy kept Gossip fit with long hacks and frequent lungeing sessions. Once a week, she drove him to dressage trainer David Hunt's school, where David tried to make some sort of sense of his flat work.

Gossip's autumn plans were to conclude with the Dutch three-day-event championships at Boekelo, scheduled for mid-October. Burghley was not considered feasible, as it would give Lucinda barely a month to re-acquaint herself with Gossip after she returned from Montreal.

At the end of July, Gossip became number one again. Be Fair slipped the tendon off the back of his hock as he jumped the final fence on the cross country at Bromont, where the Olympic three-day event was being staged. The injury put a premature end to his three-day-eventing career.

Oh how wise Lady Doreen had been when she urged Lucinda to buy Gossip. Had some premonition given her a glimpse of the future?

A miserable Be Fair hobbled back into the yard after his long flight back from Canada. It was heart-rending to see his happy, cock-sure expression reduced to one of dejection. He was put out in one of the fields to enjoy the remainder of the summer with his beloved Jupy, Lucinda's old pony, to recuperate.

But Gossip's premier position was first overshadowed and ultimately shared by a hairy hunter who arrived in the yard three weeks before Burghley. His name was Killaire. Gossip turned up his nose in disdain at such a common stablemate, all but sniggering behind Killaire's back. They were so unalike in temperament and nature it was hard to believe that they were both in the same game.

Killaire was a completely honest, open-hearted horse who never thought other than to try his best. But he did retain a certain cheek, amplified one day when I spent forty-five minutes standing in the field trying to catch him. Killaire scuttled round me in circles, just out of reach, a broad grin on his face.

Killaire was overweight when he arrived, and had to go on a crash diet, combined with some fast exercise, in order that he would be ready for Burghley.

There, he surprised other riders and the public alike, who had never heard of him, by scrabbling into second place, behind Jane Holderness-Roddam on Warrior. His owner, Charles Cyzer, was amazed and overjoyed at his horse's hitherto disguised capabilities.

Gossip ran at Dauntsey, Goodwood and Chatsworth one-day events that autumn, all sizable advanced courses. He did nothing to dislodge the faith in his cross-country ability, although he continued to battle with Lucinda over the speed at which he liked to jump. But the dressage problems were still at stalemate both in and out of the arena.

At Boekelo his dressage was indifferent, and on cross-country day Gossip received an unexpected shock at the Normandy Bank complex. He jumped up onto the bank and out over the rails which had a six-foot drop the other side. To Lucinda's horror he landed in a crumpled heap on the other side, and Lucinda stepped off. Her only conclusion was that he had never met a Normandy Bank before and the drop had taken him completely by surprise. He must have failed to put out his stabilisers.

He finished Boekelo in an ignominious twenty-fourth place, but with new-found knowledge of how to cope with Normandy Banks. It was the first and last time he forgot to operate his undercarriage.

So ended Gossip's first year in England. Lucinda, far from thinking forward to the possibilities of Badminton in 1977, was seriously wondering if the partnership was ever going to come right.

It was hard to define the year as a progressive one. Although Gossip had amassed several placings in one-day events, plus a third at Tidworth, these did not help to disguise the fact that no inroads had been made with the dressage.

The cross country, apart from Boekelo, had been consistently clear but not through harmony. Each round had been a battle from start to finish, as Lucinda tussled to try and find the pace she wanted, and Gossip fought back, insisting that it had to be flat out or not at all.

It was an inconclusive end to 1976, and left a question mark over 1977.

5   A Door is Unlocked

At the beginning of 1977, Lisa Waltman took over from me at Appleshaw when I left for a change of scene. She quickly and efficiently picked up Lucinda's methods and routine, but more importantly, she established a rapport with Gossip which he badly needed.

I had been too involved with Be Fair and Wakey throughout 1976. My allegiance, anyway, entirely belonged to Be Fair, which made life hard for Gossip as he knew that he wasn't the favoured one. He and I had rubbed along well enough but we were both a little reserved towards each other. To me he was still the 'new boy'.

So when Lisa arrived, although Gossip was number one he wasn't really enjoying the star treatment. As he had yet to really prove himself, nobody fussed over him or took particular notice of him. Lisa changed all that. Like Katie had done, Lisa's initial feelings were that she felt sorry for him. When Gossip realised he had someone's sympathies, he began to take a reciprocating interest in his new 'nanny'.

In Lisa's eyes Gossip became 'special'. Gossip lowered his guard even more, as Lisa gained his confidence and strengthened their growing mutual trust. Gossip became almost well-behaved in the stable, as he felt more secure, and he spent more time looking over the top half of his door into the yard, rather than skulking in the corner of his stable, bottom firmly planted by the door.

Lucinda, after some in-depth thought through the winter, decided that the only way she might crack a few of the problems she and Gossip had run into, was to do 'a helluva lot with him'. Gossip's incredible, virtually bottomless stamina, combined with iron-tough legs, enabled him to withstand masses of work. As Gossip was now nine, Lucinda could not afford to give him a lenient time if he was to don Be Fair's mantle.

So that spring Gossip spent many days doing dressage and show-jumping competitions, and participating in cross-country schools at Bathampton House, Wylye, home of Lord and Lady Hugh Russell, and where Lady Hugh taught cross country at all levels from novice to advanced.

When the eventing season opened, Gossip contested Crookham open intermediate, and Brigstock advanced. Lucinda had already decided to defer Gossip from Badminton, which meant that Gossip could compete all spring and head for the Bramham three-day event, held in Yorkshire at the beginning of June.

Thus the onus of challenging the toughest of events fell to Killaire, for whom Badminton seemed the natural progressive step. Nevertheless there was an underlying worry that he might not have quite the class or speed to cope with the 'Wimbledon' of eventing. Then in March a back-up to Killaire appeared in the form of George. George was owned by Mrs Elaine Straker and he was without a rider for Badminton. George had competed at Badminton before and was basically considered a very good horse, but he had occasionally blotted his copybook with an unexpected fall. This he had managed to do once at the last fence at Badminton, when ridden by Matthew Straker, who verbally registered his annoyance with one or two choice four-letter words in front of vast crowds and TV cameras.

Lisa had to redouble her affections towards Gossip when he was once again put in the shade by the two Badminton contenders, and she made sure Gossip did not suffer from any feelings of neglect.

I came back to help out over Badminton. Extra organisation was required as Lucinda had two rides, and Lisa had not experienced the machinations behind the scenes of a three-day event.

On the Saturday night of Badminton, Lisa and I could not believe the results. George was lying first and Killaire third. On Sunday I watched George show-jump, wound up with

apprehension, not that he might hit a rail but that he would
suffer the same fate as Wakey. The terrible end to Badminton
'76 was still fresh in my mind. It seemed unbelievable that a
year had passed since the tragedy. I hoped that it was an
impossibility, against the law of averages, that such a horror
should happen a second time, but fate does deal out some
bizarre and frightening cards.

George was fine. He and Killaire both jumped clear and
kept their places, divided by Diana Thorne on her brilliant
grey, The Kingmaker. As I led George down to the Whitbread
tent for his official photographs, Lisa generously commented,
'There, he is finishing off Badminton '76 for you and Wakey.'

Two weeks later, Lucinda fell victim, literally, to the
hazardous side of eventing, when she broke her collar-bone in
a fall with Hysterical at the Locko Park one-day event on May
1st. An anxious Lisa suddenly had the responsibility thrust on
her of driving the now larger, four-horsebox back down to
Hampshire on her own, and she had only practised driving it a
few times.

Lucinda's iron-willed determination, along with various
therapeutic treatments, welded the collar-bone back together
in time for Gossip's trip to Bramham.

At Bramham Gossip's dressage was mediocre. His tests had
stabilised onto a plateau, whereby the marks neither plum-
meted nor indicated any radical improvement.

The next day, on the roads and tracks, Gossip was a
nightmare, even worse than the year before at Tidworth.
Lucinda and he came off phase C puffing and sweating,
Lucinda feeling nearly as exhausted as Katie had at Burghley.
As Lucinda set off on the cross country she couldn't help
wondering how Katie had *ever* managed him when he was
younger, for then he must have been even more impossible.
On the cross country, Gossip caused a minor upset by
incurring twenty penalties for a stop at a simple shark's-teeth
fence on top of a hill. Lucinda blamed herself entirely for this
mishap, feeling she had not helped to set him up at the corner
before the sharp turn into the fence. Gossip had scooted left
and slid past it, having not received any positive instructions
from his rider. It was so hard to know quite what to do with

Gossip when a fence loomed ahead; he always fought any assistance from Lucinda but obviously he did need guidance.

Despite his stop, Gossip still finished in fifth place after the show-jumping, his very fast time cross country helping to keep his penalty points down.

While at Bramham, Lucinda bumped into Katie who was thrilled to see her Goose looking so well and happy.

Lucinda asked Katie the question that had been whirring in her brain, 'How did she manage him?' Katie laughed and smilingly said she thought that really Gossip managed himself. She had never been able to have any say in the matter as Gossip pulled so hard.

Coincidentally, friends had told Lucinda that they could not understand why she bothered with such a screw-ball as Gossip when there were so many other horses around that she could have ridden. But, like Katie, Lucinda was determined to carry on. Somewhere, somehow, there had to be an answer to this brilliant, yet temperamental horse.

Lucinda envied Katie's position of an 'unknown' in the eventing world, where there is so much less pressure if one has a difficult horse to cope with in public. Because of Lucinda's fame, people expected her to be virtually perfect at each appearance, which doubled the pressures when a horse like Gossip was involved.

Lucinda was pleased with Gossip at Bramham, not over-concerned at their cross-country mistake, but she did not allow him a long, lazy summer holiday. After a two-week break, Lucinda planned to take Gossip to Germany to top dressage trainer, Herbert Rehbein, for a week's tuition. That was to be followed by Gossip's second three-day event, the Luhmühlen CCI, where Be Fair had gained his European victory two years before.

At Rehbein's, Lucinda became even more demoralised when Gossip went quite beautifully for Herbert. Herbert even went so far as to say he would have had Gossip for his own dressage horse if he had been a little bigger. Rehbein had somehow found a secret key to Gossip, but Lucinda could not discover the correct combination to open the safe in Gossip's mind. Herbert helped Lucinda enormously and she absorbed many ideas. But, looking back, Lucinda sees that she never really understood that she could neither tell nor ask Gossip to come onto the bit. Herbert, through his natural balance, had intuitively *felt* this with Gossip and had ridden him accordingly. So Gossip, of his own volition, had quietly started to co-operate and do some superb dressage. But it is far more difficult to try and impart this feel to a rider who is desperately searching for the answer.

Nevertheless, Gossip's test in Luhmühlen was a big improvement on Bramham. Herbert had generously lent Lucinda his own dressage saddle that was so well moulded, Lucinda found it a joy to ride in. In fact, so good did she look that one of the dressage judges was misguidedly impressed and awarded Gossip twenty marks more than either of the other two. Gossip lay an unprecedented fifth at the end of the day. His mark incensed one rival competitor so much that he demanded the score be amended, or he would withdraw his horses from the event. But Gossip's mark remained and so did he, and the judge in question kept a nervous low profile until the fuss had died down.

To Lucinda's horror, the sixth and seventh fences on the cross-country course comprised a water complex, entailing a jump into water off a Normandy Bank. The last such fence Gossip had tackled, had been at Boekelo. Lucinda felt sure she was in for a ducking.

After his usual exhaustive antics round the first three phases, Gossip bounded off onto phase D. As he took off over the rail of the Normandy Bank, Lucinda sat back, waiting for the sensation of cold water penetrating her clothes. She never felt so much as a drop. Gossip landed safely, with professional aplomb, and cantered out and away to the next fence. Lucinda's estimation of him shot up several notches. Then at fence eight, a big tree-trunk slung across a gaping ditch, he showed a complete antithesis of character, when he spooked violently before flinging himself across the obstacle.

At his sudden stop-start action, Lucinda was ejected forward out of the saddle, but clung on with her feet somewhere near the pommel, and her knees touching, in the manner of a jump jockey. Happily, over the rest of the course he was more consistent and they finished clear. He spooked too, throughout his show-jumping round the following day, but again managed to go clear and kept the second place he had moved up to, chiefly due to his fast time on the cross country.

Back on English soil Gossip was allowed a three-week break and took a back seat until after the European Championships at Burghley, where Lucinda was partnering George in the defence of her title and also as part of the British team. It was a dramatic Burghley. Lucinda was suffering from a mysterious bug that made her feel weak and very tired. On the steeplechase, George caught his foot in some trailing string marking the course. He tripped badly and Lucinda flew over his head. George recovered and galloped on, towing Lucinda who was clinging to the reins. Pleas of 'Whoa, George!' from Lucinda broke through his oblivion and he slowed to a stop. Lucinda hauled herself back on board, feeling like the proverbial dishcloth, and finished the course. Because her fall was outside the penalty zones, they were clear, and miraculously, without time penalties. On phase D, shrugging off encroaching exhaustion from the fall, the 'bug' and George's strong relentless pull, Lucinda steered George to another clear round, and ultimately to a second European title. The team also rewarded the enthusiastic home crowd with a British victory.

George had done all and more than anyone had hoped or expected. Lucinda bade him an emotional farewell as he left for his home in Yorkshire that evening with the Strakers.

In the year that followed, George was gradually retired from the eventing scene, and his career mellowed to the hunting field where he found equal thrills following hounds.

Gossip and Killaire kept Lucinda occupied for the remainder of the autumn season. Gossip was technically second at Buckleberry, but was eliminated when Lucinda forgot to weigh in at the end of the cross country. Possibly the champagne bubbles were still fizzing in her brain from the recent Burghley celebrations.

The next weekend Gossip ran at an open hunter trial in

which competitors were required to open and shut a gate. Gossip's patience grew very thin as Lucinda fumbled with the latch, and he almost jumped it in exasperation. To make up for any lost time, Gossip scorched round the rest of the course and clinched first place. A happy side story to that hunter trial was the re-emergence of Be Fair, now recovered as much as could be hoped from his hock injury. His eyes lit up and he galloped round the course, revelling in his favourite pastime, and his contented expression showed his happiness when Lucinda tied his third-prize rosette to his headcollar.

Gossip put on some more mileage at Goodwood advanced, and then I joined up with him again for the rest of the season, as Lisa had flown to the States with Killaire, who was to compete with Lucinda at the Ledyard three-day event in early October.

Whilst Killaire was undergoing the compulsory two-day quarantine in America, I drove Gossip and Be Fair down to Knowlton horse trials in Kent. Gossip and Lucinda underlined their growing confidence in each other and collected another second. Be Fair was not placed but he was happy enough just to be a part of the scene again.

As soon as Knowlton was over, Lucinda flew to the States to join Lisa and Killaire. I stayed on at Appleshaw to pack Gossip's luggage and escort him to Boekelo.

The day after we arrived at Boekelo, Lucinda appeared, having successfully ridden Killaire over a huge course at Ledyard. Killaire had pushed himself to the limit in order to go clear. For a horse that was not designed to event, he was magnificent, and completely deserved his hard-won third place, behind the linchpin of American teams, Mike Plumb, who took first and second places on his own two rides.

Once again, at Boekelo Gossip's dressage was not worth any notable comments, save that he wasn't last, but he still left himself a large leeway to make up on the cross country. This he did in no uncertain terms, finishing almost a minute inside the time allowed. In those days a fast round at Boekelo was one where a rider came home with fifteen or twenty time faults. Gossip was just being his usual impossible, uncontrollable, fast self. The lack of time faults, in his case, was incidental. By the end of the show-jumping, Gossip had sneaked up to second place again behind Horst Karsten's Sioux, who had been responsible for keeping him at bay at Luhmühlen in July.

Although the cross country was still a fight over pace, and the dressage showed little appreciable difference, Lucinda felt more familiar with Gossip and reasonably optimistic for 1978.

Gossip also had helped to create an incredible and memorable year for Lucinda and Lisa, as George, Gossip and Killaire between them had lifted Lucinda to almost invincible heights, and offset the sadness and disappointments of 1976.

Looking ahead to 1978, Lucinda could seriously contemplate Gossip's entry for Badminton now that they were forming a definite partnership, although Lucinda was still concerned over how to control his frightening speed when faced with the Badminton fences. Somehow she would have to resolve that problem. Badminton, otherwise, was unthinkable.

Only six weeks into 1978, one of the happiest and most welcome events occurred at Appleshaw. On February 14th, Overseas Containers Ltd wholeheartedly offered their support to Lucinda by becoming the first sponsors of an event rider.

The costs of feeding, training and competing event horses were reaching staggering proportions. The situation was becoming grave enough, particularly since the death of the General the previous summer, to necessitate Lucinda having to give up if a sponsor could not be found.

OCL, of which company the General had once been a director, stepped into the breach. As Lucinda said, 'It was my best Valentine ever.'

In January, Lucinda took Gossip, Killaire and a novice, Botany Bay, to a dressage course at Stoneleigh given by Ernst Bachinger, who had trained at the Spanish Riding School in Vienna. For the next three years, Ernst was to offer much valued guidance and advice in his official capacity as trainer to the British team, wherein he dramatically improved the dressage performances.

Lucinda enjoyed a constructive week with Ernst, who assessed Gossip's problems and Lucinda's riding, and suggested she needed a much deeper seat in the saddle before a reliable test could be produced. Consequently, Lucinda found herself on the lunge each day without stirrups, which was an enormous help. But the course did not really solve many of Gossip's problems, and unfortunately Ernst did not particularly like Gossip, which did not start them off on a very good footing.

There were by now quite a few young horses at Appleshaw and Lucinda found she was having increasingly less time to do them justice, and she started to scout around for a co-jockey. Long-time friend William Micklem suggested his brother Charlie.

Charlie came to Appleshaw from Bertie Hill's training yard in Devon, where he was head lad. Although he had no previous experience of eventing, other than at Pony Club level, he was an accomplished National Hunt jockey and had ridden a wide variety of horses in point-to-points and 'chases with considerable success.

Charlie is a completely natural rider and always looks at one with his horse, knowing intuitively how best to handle a horse after only a few moments in the saddle. Charlie's calm, unflappable temperament was at a premium on nervous excitable thoroughbreds, which were the type Charlie most enjoyed riding.

Charlie proved himself within six months, by competing in and winning his first three-day event, at Bramham, that June. There he was riding in one of the novice sections on a 15.3 hh threequarter-bred horse called Liverpool Bay, named after one of OCL's container ships, as were most of the horses now at Appleshaw – except Gossip, who was too infamous to have his name changed.

Liverpool Bay was not going to make a top-class eventer but he nevertheless gave Charlie a rocket-like boost to his eventing career.

Gossip's fitness work was proving a problem. The previous autumn, Lucinda had found him impossible to work out conventionally, as he had fought and plunged against the bit, every step of the work-out. His incessant pulling kept making his mouth sore, and he lost weight from the excess energy he was expending. No matter how boring Lucinda made the canters, Gossip always wanted to go faster. The only time Gossip would ever canter properly was in the school.

So Lucinda changed tactics and resorted to trot work up varying gradients of hill, combined with an occasional fast gallop up a slope to tighten his muscles and clear his wind. This method, plus the events, had produced Gossip at peak fitness for Boekelo, and Lucinda hoped the system would work again this spring as Gossip was being as difficult as ever.

Gossip filled nobody with any optimism at his first event at Crookham. He began his dressage test with a rear then reversed rapidly at his supposed halt at X. On the cross country Lucinda tried more determinedly than ever to govern Gossip's approach to the fences. Forcing him to slow down for a sharp right-hand turn into some rails, Gossip's answer was to slam to a halt. He also ran out at the following fence. Gossip was not going to stand for any sort of domination. If he could not have his own way then he was not going to operate at all.

Lucinda was in despair. The culmination of two years of trying to persuade Gossip to listen had resulted in a stop at one of the easiest fences at Crookham. Badminton was only five weeks away and Gossip was her only contender, as Killaire had contracted an infection in a front leg and had been sent back to Charles Cyzer's home in Sussex to convalesce.

OCL's introduction to and hopes for the most important three-day event on the calendar lay on the shoulders of one horse and Lucinda still had no idea if he had the ability, will, obedience and temperament to take on the course, let alone complete it. For Lucinda, the pressures and responsibilities to the new sponsors were almost overwhelming.

The week following Crookham, Gossip knocked himself, and his fitness work took a very diverse route, when he was swum round the circular pool at nearby Lambourn, to maintain his condition while his leg recovered.

His next event was Rushall. The going was wet, which

didn't suit him as he tended to become bogged down in mud, and needed even more speed to propel himself over the fences. In deference to the state of the ground, and in total despair that the long struggle to try and ride Gossip conventionally had ended in a refusal at Crookham, Lucinda felt she had no alternative. On the cross country, she eased the reins and let him go at the speed he wanted. He won the class. Whilst other riders motored steadily through the mud, Gossip sped flat out into his fences, never making any semblance of a mistake, and coped brilliantly while his rider remained totally passive. As she pulled up, after crossing the finish, it dawned on Lucinda what fantastic courage and confidence he must have, not to need help from the rider, and to put his entire concentration onto the fence in front of him. If she had not been so desperate, she would not have dared risk allowing him such freedom, but it had been the only avenue left open to her and she had left him completely alone. Gossip had responded by giving Lucinda one of the safest and most inspired rides ever. Rushall was a major turning point and from that day on, Gossip was ridden no other way.

But this revolutionary new way of riding Gossip had only been tested once, and his next event was Badminton. Lucinda could not quite believe that he would cope with the bigger fences and combinations without rider interference. She could not seriously envisage galloping round the course doing absolutely nothing.

Doubts and worries filled the days in the run-up to Badminton. The positive and inspired tingling of nerves, as the adrenalin begins to run, were noticeably lacking and Lucinda's confidence wobbled as though on a slackened tight-rope. Badminton was *the* event where sponsors could literally fly their flag. If Lucinda and Gossip failed to meet the challenge, letting OCL down in these early crucial months when it was vital to make a good impression, sponsorship and possible team selection could disappear down the drain in one quick swoosh.

Lady Doreen, always quickly sensitive to a situation, was aware of the anxious indecisive thoughts. On the morning of the cross country at Badminton she wrote Lucinda a note that helped inspire the necessary aggression, and expose the positive aspect: the challenge of riding Gossip against the coursebuilder Col. Frank Weldon, who that year had designed one of the bigger Badmintons. It was a challenge Lucinda had not considered. It was what she needed to motivate herself into forward gear.

After a 'good for Gossip' dressage, Gossip was twenty points behind the dressage leader that year, Jane Starkey and Topper Too. Coincidentally his mark was 66.8 and he was in eighteenth place, as he had been with Katie at Burghley in 1975. His position was the equivalent of one refusal or a handful of time faults behind the leader. The added incentive of the will to win succeeded in charging up the rest of Lucinda's batteries.

First to go, Gossip was watched by hundreds of pairs of eyes as Lisa loosed him off onto phase A, in front of the gracious façade of Badminton House.

Up on the wind-swept field of phase B, Gossip nearly reared Lucinda off at the start of the steeplechase. His nerves, like Be Fair's, had overcome him at the start of each phase, and if he did not have the reassurance of someone leading him to the start flags, he would, like his chestnut predecessor, whip round and nap before the countdown had even begun. At Badminton, as the starting steward counted 'Three . . .' Gossip stood up on end, unable to contain himself, forelegs flailing close to Lisa's head as she held the lead rein that she would slide out from the bit rings on the word 'Go!' Lucinda flung her arms around Gossip's neck to stop herself sliding over his tail. Lisa hastily slackened off the lead rein, and as Gossip's front feet came back to earth, she slipped the rein from the bit-rings, timing it perfectly with the command 'Go!' from the starter. Lucinda, still unbalanced, frantically grabbed at the reins as Gossip pelted towards the first of the steeplechase fences. They finished safely, well within the time. Lucinda had given up trying to steady him on the 'chase. They took more out of each other, fighting, so Gossip went at his own speed, and often finished half or even threequarters of a minute inside the time allowed.

Fifty minutes later, the loudspeakers echoed across the

Park, 'Number one, OCL's Village Gossip, ridden by Lucinda Prior-Palmer, is away at a great gallop to the first fence.'

Gossip had never seen such big fences before. And the size of them did nothing but make him go better. Respecting their size, Gossip, unhindered by his rider, set himself up for each approach just that little bit earlier than he normally did, giving himself time to analyse the problems each fence presented. Lucinda disciplined herself to sit still. By using her weight distribution and balance, she was able to indicate changes of pace or direction without over-use of the reins, which might cause a fight. Her rein contact was hardly more than incidental. Gossip revelled in the freedom. At an exhilarating pace, he flashed over the fences with derisive dismissal. He galloped through the finish at the same incredible speed with which he had started, and received a terrific cheer from his supporters, who knew of the anxieties that had been involved. He was clear and forty-five seconds inside the time, the only horse that day to finish without time faults.

By the end of the day Gossip had been overtaken by only one horse, Warrior, victor of last year's Burghley and who had been lying second behind Topper, the latter having dropped down the order with some time faults. There was even an official complaint lodged with the ground jury on Saturday evening, when, unknown to the Prior-Palmers, someone thought Warrior should be penalised for a stop, as he had hesitated on top of the quarry complex. However, after the ground jury had watched a re-run of the film taken by the BBC, they decided it was merely a hesitation and not a stop, which would have given Warrior a very costly twenty penalties and put him below Gossip.

On Sunday Warrior and Gossip both jumped clear and retained their positions. Lucinda was overjoyed and also intensely relieved. It was only after it was all over that she knew her primary worry had been that OCL should be able to witness a successful first Badminton and not a shambolic disaster.

OCL were thrilled at the outcome. Ronald Swayne, chairman of OCL, even went so far as to state, 'If Village

Gossip polishes up his manners in the dressage arena, we will nominate him OCL man of the year!'

Gossip didn't quite make 'man of the year', but his superlative showing across country at Badminton put him onto the short-list, along with Killaire, for the World Championships that September.

6 *World Championships, Lexington*

The USA was to be the host country for the 1978 World Championships. The venue was the famous Kentucky Horse Park at Lexington, in the heart of the Blue Grass country. The date chosen for the Championships was mid-September, which coincided with the official opening of the Horse Park.

Gossip, after a lazy two months among the buttercups, was brought back into work on June 10th. Killaire, now fully recovered from his leg problems, returned to Appleshaw to prepare, with Gossip, for the two selection trials.

The first trial was at Dauntsey in the first week of August. Gossip surprised everyone by producing a fairly relaxed test. Mrs Allhusen, one of the judges, was so amazed at his performance that she gave him some good marks. Lucinda was well aware that it was sheer fluke rather than any technical improvement that had ordained Gossip to perform a civilised test. She was still no further forward in her quest for the answer to unlock the secret to Gossip's mind. If Gossip felt like being kind and genial, he was. If he didn't want to co-operate, he told the world, and Lucinda could only sit and suffer the humiliating consequences.

So at Dauntsey, Gossip felt agreeable. He reinforced his dressage with a fast, clear cross country and a clean show-jumping round, and finished second to his fellow rival at Burghley, Gurgle the Greek, who was as unbeatable as ever in the dressage phase.

Killaire, determined not to be left out of the picture, scuttled round the course after a good dressage to win the other advanced section.

Metaphorically patting themselves on the backs, a very

smug Gossip and Killaire were driven up to Locko, two weeks later, for the second and final trial. Gossip was bubbling with good spirits and he over-fizzed in the dressage, unable to keep the cork from popping, and consequently earned himself a set of fairly disparaging marks from the judges.

Through the year, Gossip's cross country had ricocheted from being resentful and erratic at Crookham in the spring, to a state of sublime overconfidence by Locko. He stood off at several fences, instead of chipping in with a short stride or two before take-off, and started to become a little flippant. As he came out of the water jump, he all but landed in a heap as he had not bothered to give himself enough time to size up the three-foot sleeper bank out. He breasted the bank and, luckily, his impetus landed him on top of it, but only his cat-like agility and quick brain kept him on his feet. It was one of the very rare occasions that Gossip actually did make a silly mistake.

Despite his unorthodox cross country and bad dressage, he still managed to come sixth. Killaire, although lying second after the dressage, knocked a rail in the show-jumping, added another seven time penalties across country, and ended up seventh.

The next morning all the short-listed horses were trotted up in front of Peter Scott-Dunn, the team vet, Tadzik Kopanski, chef d'équipe, and the selection committee. When it was their turn, Gossip and Killaire strode out looking sound and fit. The team was chosen, and Lucinda was one of the members. She elected Gossip as her partner, with Killaire travelling out as reserve. Reports coming back from Lexington indicated that the weather could be hot and humid, Kentucky being in the central part of the States. As Gossip had limitless stamina and was an altogether tougher horse, he seemed the logical choice. It was only after the Championships, with the benefit of hindsight, that Lucinda wondered if she had chosen correctly.

So at the end of August, the team, consisting of Lucinda with Gossip and Killaire, Chris Collins with Smokey, Jane Holderness-Roddam with Badminton hero Warrior, and Richard Meade on the 'Gossip look-alike' Bleak Hills, gathered at Bathampton House, Wylye, for the last week of training before flying out to America. They were joined by the two nominated individual riders, Jane Starkey with Topper Too, who had been reserve horse at Montreal, and Lizzie Boone (now Purbrick) with the powerfully strong Felday Farmer.

Ernst Bachinger was at Wylye to help brush up the dressage and sort out any last-minute problems. But with Gossip, Ernst was at a loss. The horse was one big headache, and Ernst could not find a way to break through to him. Ernst's method of riding was brilliant but dominating, and, of course, Gossip could not and would not accept his hand and leg when Ernst rode him. Lucinda's hopes for Gossip's dressage hit a new low ebb. If a rider as talented and disciplined as Ernst could not fathom Gossip, how could she ever hope to come close to a conciliation with her explosive black fireball?

Ernst, for lack of any other ideas, suggested sending Gossip round the school loose, without a rider, but wearing tight side-reins, in the hopes of obtaining some submission. Lucinda was willing to try anything, so Gossip was driven round the indoor school at trot and canter, encouraged forward with the tactful use of lunge whips. The ruse made no appreciable difference. Gossip, remembering his days at Ashbrooke, was comfortable in the side-reins and did not fight them, but then neither did he completely give to them, and despite his outline looking better there was still tension throughout his body.

Lucinda continued to go through the motions of schooling him and Gossip tensed up, hollowing his back and shortening his stride as he felt Lucinda say, 'Come here, listen to me.' The fitter he became the more loth he was to contemplate accepting discipline, and the more he was pressurised, the more fractious and annoyed he became. His dressage had reached an impasse.

At 1.15 am on a Sunday morning, 10 days before the Championships, horses and grooms left Wylye for Gatwick airport; the riders were to follow on a few days later. It was a long flight for the horses with the plane stopping off in Cologne to pick up the German and Dutch teams' horses. Gossip and his team-mates travelled well, their chief objections being to the take-offs and landings, when the engines roared and they had to brace themselves against the gradient of the ascents and descents.

All livestock entering the USA has to undergo a period of quarantine, the length dependent on the country from whence the animal originated. Horses coming in from Europe were usually released after two days, assuming that blood tests taken on arrival were in order. Under normal circumstances all animals go to the quarantine station near New York, but for the World Championships a special quarantine station was set up, two and a half hours' drive from Cincinnati airport and only two to three miles from their ultimate destination, Kentucky Horse Park. What was more, grooms could stay with and look after their horses in quarantine, which is not permitted under normal regulations.

The temporary quarantine stables were spacious and cool, a comfortable haven from the promised high temperatures and pressing humidity that prevailed outside.

The morning after their arrival, September 3rd, Lisa and her fellow grooms led the horses out for a short leg-stretch, and, in the cool of the evening, a gentle lunge to loosen their muscles. None of their charges showed any sign of ill-effects from the journey, and they were beginning to adapt to the ninety-degree temperatures.

On the 5th the horses were officially released from quarantine, and moved to their new quarters. The stabling at Kentucky was in one enormous barn. Large, roomy looseboxes lined each side of the walls. Down the centre, were smaller temporary stables that had been erected to house the individuals and to serve as tack and feed rooms.

As the horses began to fill the stables in the barn, their collective body-heat raised the temperature inside still further. It was like walking about in a giant oven. Lisa clipped Gossip, as did others in an effort to allow the horses the maximum chance of keeping cool, but Lisa found Gossip's summer coat so fine there was very little to clip off. Chris Collins found a more practical solution: he bought Smokey an electrically powered fan to hang high on the wall of his box. His idea quickly caught on, and soon nearly all the horses in the barn had a fan, under which they stood happily, enjoying the relief from the leaden air.

As the days passed the horses acclimatised to the stagnant heat, but extra salt was added to their feed to combat that lost from heavier sweating and to encourage drinking to offset the risk of dehydration in the vapid conditions.

The riders worked the horses early in the morning, around 6 am, so they could rest during the heat of the day. Many other teams adopted this policy, but not the Canadians. They worked their horses at a more normal hour, which at first seemed a little tough, but they did have a point. The horses were being worked in conditions which, unless the weather changed, would be similar to those on the competition days.

Lucinda found Gossip was impervious to the heat, and his sharp bristling attitude to work had not been sapped in any way by the soporific conditions. On work-out days, Gossip was in his usual fighting form, and caused some mixed looks of horror and amusement from the American contingent.

Since 1974 Lucinda had been an enthusiastic follower of the interval training programme that the American riders had used for some years to fitten their horses. But for Gossip the method was too disciplined and Lucinda was still utilising her own personal plan for him. Thus other competitors would see a small black horse scampering across the park at a very fast trot, head in the air and nose poked out, as Lucinda sat quietly, trying to rise rhythmically to his erratic trot, reins flapping in loops.

Whilst the American riders meticulously measured out their horses' paces and worked their horses precisely to the stopwatch, keeping a steady or slowly increasing pace, they would suddenly be passed by a flash of black as Gossip zoomed up a slope in the manner of an out-of-control racehorse, as he snaked between the other competitors. But many roads lead to Rome, and Lucinda was utterly confident that Gossip was 110 per cent fit for the task required of him.

The course at Kentucky was huge, one of the biggest Lucinda had ever seen. Designed by international US event rider Roger Haller, it had been constructed from the finest timber, and Rick Newton, the coursebuilder, had every reason to be proud of his work. Each fence had its problems, but none, at first impression, seemed insurmountable. The overriding concern most competitors shared was how to cope with the course as a whole. The cumulative effects of jumping and galloping over four and threequarter miles in hot, humid conditions could prove severely taxing. The technical delegate assigned to approve the course, Wolfgang Feld, and the ground jury certainly envisaged this possibility and reduced phase C by threequarters of a mile, though allowing the horses the same time to complete it. It wasn't much of a reduction but it would help. And as Jock Ferrie, chef d'équipe to the lone Irish representative, John Watson, said, 'This isn't a bloody Pony Club trot, it's the World Championships.'

The going itself was good with no rough ground, steep hills, or sudden twists and turns to negotiate. Jock had a point. Gathered at Kentucky were the cream of the eventing world. The gauntlet had been thrown down and the challenge offered.

On September 13th, the 1978 World Championships rolled into action. In fact they started with a deluge, as a drenching monsoon broke suddenly in the middle of the vets' inspection, which was being held on a road below the stables. Chaos reigned as horses, riders, grooms, officials and spectators fled to the big barn for shelter. It was there that the inspection resumed, with riders jogging their horses down the aisles, trying to avoid the paraphernalia of tack, trunks and other stable equipment.

Gossip was number 3 and first to go for the British team, so his dressage test was timed for Thursday morning. Lucinda had tried hard not to niggle and irritate him whilst schooling. Ernst, who was on hand, understandingly did not offer his services, knowing there was nothing he could say that would transform Gossip's dressage.

Frank Weldon, one of the ground jury at Kentucky, accurately summed up Gossip in one of his reports for *Horse and Hound* magazine: 'Village Gossip is undoubtedly brilliant at cross country, and on his day can do a fair test. The trouble is, it is impossible to forecast how the spirit will move him on the first day, for his whole outline can change in a flash if the least thing upsets him.' This was Gossip in a nutshell; always he would have the final say.

As it turned out, Gossip compromised. Although never really on the bit he was neither explosive nor spooky. One or two kind spectators even suggested he had been harshly marked. Whether it was the heat or that he was in a mellow mood, his test earned him a passable 70.4. Maybe for him it was a tough mark, but compared to the other competitors' tests, Lucinda felt it was fair as Gossip's dressage was a long way short of world-class standard. Even so, by the end of the first day, Gossip lay third behind the title holder, Bruce Davidson, this time mounted on his young grey, Might Tango, who had 61.4; in second place lay one of the Dutchmen, Huub Jansson on Kimbel.

But on the second day, some very impressive tests pushed the first-day leaders into the shade. Three German riders produced precise, accurate dressage with scores in the fifties, as did two US riders and top Dutch rider Eddie Stibbe. But three Brits kept the Union Jack flying high, as Bleak Hills, Topper and Warrior also scored below sixty, doing great credit to Ernst. Warrior's test was a delight to watch, elegant and flowing, and Jane earned rapturous applause and a mark of 52.

But it was the American team captain, Mike Plumb, on his Ledyard winner Laurenson, who took the lead after two days of dressage with a supremely polished test that put them 1.8 points ahead of Jane.

These scores pushed Gossip back to twenty-fourth place, but still only the equivalent of a refusal behind the leader. And with a course as tough as everyone was predicting, anything could happen. It did . . .

Gossip started phase A at 10.12 am. The day had begun cloudy and breezy with a damp coolness to the humid air, a minor miracle after days of scorching sun in an empty sky. But would it last? everyone was asking.

Gossip jiggled his way through phase A, and burst onto phase B. At the threequarter mark Lucinda glanced at her watch and misread it. Thinking that Gossip, despite his speed, might collect time faults, she gave him a little more of his head. Gossip streaked away and through the finish. It was only as they pulled up that Lucinda realised her mistake. He was a minute inside the time. Cursing to herself at the unnecessary waste of energy, Lucinda let Gossip recover his breath on phase C, and by the time they reached the vet Box before phase D, he was his pulling, bouncing self and looked as fresh as ever.

While Lisa sponged Gossip down, Tadzik relayed to Lucinda what news he could about the course. At this early stage there was virtually none and what there was, was not good. Kimbel, who had been in front of Gossip after the dressage, had retired on the 'chase. The second rider, an Argentinian, had already fallen at fence three, the Pavillion, but was continuing.

As the bleeps died away, Lucinda and Gossip stormed out of the start of phase D. He was sensational. As fence after fence rose up and then diminished behind them, Lucinda felt he had never galloped nor jumped so brilliantly. Soon they were approaching fence fourteen, Fort Lexington, which comprised a wide ditch onto the face of a steep ten-foot bank, at the top of which was an 'in and out' followed by an equally sharp descent down the other side.

As Lucinda and Gossip drew near, they could see the luckless Argentinian in front of them, pulling his horse out of the ditch. He had suffered a second fall at fence thirteen, the comparatively insignificant hors d'oeuvre to Fort Lexington, and this third fall at the Fort now eliminated him. He and his horse stood to one side as Gossip flashed past to launch himself onto the bank. Gossip bounded up to the top in two leaps, propelled himself over the in and out, skipped down the other side and streamed away to the next fence. He was the first horse to have made it this far and thus to chart the rest of the course.

'What an incredible horse,' thought Lucinda, elated at the nonchalant and positive way Gossip had tackled the Fort. Riding him was akin to driving a Ferrari, but with rather less responsive brakes. Lucinda knew there was no way she could slow down his furious gallop, and she prayed his stamina would take him to the finish. The cloud cover of the morning had lifted, and the sun was cooking up the temperatures, dragging the humidity level with them.

Then, at the top of a rise, eight fences from home, Gossip drew a deep breath. Lucinda was suddenly aware the plug was beginning to work loose in his enormous depths of staying-power. As they cantered down the hill to the next fence, Lucinda's anxiety increased: she realised she had control for the first time on the course. This could only mean Gossip was tiring. Ahead of them lay a complex of rails zig-zagging along a meandering, water-filled ditch. They had reached the Serpent.

Lucinda closed her legs against Gossip's sides and steered him onto her chosen line through the three elements of the fence. Gossip cleared the first part, the rails over the ditch. At the second part the ground fell away sharply on take-off and the landing was on the face of a bank. Gossip made a huge effort and landed safely on the other side, but the jump had dissipated all his impulsion. For the third element, the landing was actually in water, and the line Lucinda was taking required great impulsion and a fresh horse. She had neither. Gossip hit the rails hard, and cartwheeled over them with a sickening splash into the few inches of muddy water beyond. Panic gripped Lucinda as she struggled to rise. Her head was under water and she could not move as Gossip was on top of her. After what seemed an eternity, but which was probably little more than a few seconds, Lucinda felt his weight shift, and she pulled herself up, gasping for fresh air. A bedraggled Gossip stood beside her. He was plastered in gritty silt, and was shaking his head trying to dislodge the water from his ears, an unhappy, questioning expression on his face. Lucinda leant against him, assailed overwhelmingly by the crushing feeling of letting down her team, her country, and, most of all, Gossip. It was like all motion and emotion had slammed into a brick wall, leaving a stinging numbness. Then someone ran towards her, a bright, cheery smile on her face. Sandy Brookes, an English event rider, had come out to Lexington to support the team. Sandy sploshed into the murky water. 'Don't worry, on you get,' she consoled a wet and muddy Lucinda, as she legged her up back onto Gossip.

Lucinda focused her mind back to the practical realities of

having to complete the course for the team. Picking up the reins, she headed a weary Gossip towards the remaining eight fences.

Those last few fences required more monumental effort than all the earlier fences put together. The fall had virtually drained what was left of Gossip's resources. It was his heart and his indomitable courage, which as ever refused to quit, that helped him climb laboriously over the last few jumps to the end. As Lucinda and Gossip cantered through the finish flags of phase D, Tadzik, waiting anxiously, thought they were the Argentinian pair, so unrecognisable were they from the mud of the Serpent.

After Lucinda had weighed in, and Lisa, almost shaking with relief that Gossip had returned intact, had taken Gossip off for a bath, Lucinda walked over to Tadzik to offer him what advice she could about the course, for him to pass on to the other British riders. Personally, the experience had left Lucinda with a bitter taste. If she had not been in the team, she would not have asked Gossip to continue after his fall. Although Gossip had not been injured and had somehow coped with the final fences, it had been an unfair favour to ask of a tired horse. Lucinda hated herself for pushing him to the finish. She had done it only for the sake of the team. It was after this that she seriously began to consider the possibilities of injustice to the horse when involved in team competitions at three-day events. For Lucinda, Gossip had more than proved himself to be of world-class calibre.

As the heat and humidity relentlessly increased, the later horses found the conditions more and more taxing. The Serpent, coming as it did near the end of the course, caught out another sixteen competitors and caused the retirement or elimination of nine, including Warrior and Smokey. Warrior had already had a disastrous time at fence seventeen, the first part of the Head of the Lake complex, incurring a stop and two falls. With Jane and Chris both out of the competition, the hopes of the British team collapsed. Richard and Bleak Hills escaped unscathed but for a stop at the maze, two fences from home. Lizzie was desperately unlucky to fall at the straight-forward open water, having just survived capitulation to the murk of the Serpent's water. It was left to Jane and Topper Too to keep British spirits from flagging, and they excelled themselves, achieving one of only eight clear rounds the entire day. Nobody had avoided collecting time penalties. Gossip had defied all laws of reasoning and had gained the fastest time of the day, with just 8.4 time penalties in spite of his fall. But it was Topper's round that made Lucinda wonder, in retrospect, if Killaire would have fared better than his stable-mate. Topper, no speed merchant, had been guided round the course at a steady pace by Jane. He had finished a lot less tired than many others, and despite 72 time faults, finished ninth. Gossip, incredibly, was only two places behind at eleventh.

The course had also knocked out the Dutch, New Zealand and Argentinian teams, leaving only the Americans, Germans and Canadians to fight out the team medals.

Stops and falls had decimated the American riders. Dressage leaders, Mike Plumb and Laurenson, fell victim to the Serpent and were eliminated. Two other US team members had falls, but Bruce Davidson conjured a clear round out of Might Tango, who finished the course exhausted but recovered quickly from prompt veterinary assistance, and took the lead, thus poised to capture his second world title crown.

The Germans had coped well and were still able to field a team for Sunday. But it was the Canadians who surprised everyone, ending up with a staggering lead of over a hundred points from the Americans, who lay only two points ahead of the Germans.

On that Saturday evening there were many tired horses, and devoted grooms stayed up keeping watchful vigil. Late into the night, riders checked on their mounts, and team vets constantly monitored temperatures, pulses and respiration rates.

For the first time in his life, Gossip was really tired, beyond even the bad-tempered stage. On Sunday morning he trotted up and passed the vets' inspection, but he wasn't his usual buoyant self. Back in his stable, later that morning, he suddenly began to pant like a dog. Peter Scott-Dunn was concerned and Lucinda immediately withdrew him from the show-jumping. After all he had gone through the previous day, Lucinda was disappointed that he would not be able to enjoy his just rewards of finishing his first world championships but, always, Lucinda put her horses first, and if Gossip was not feeling right then he was not going to be asked to jump it. Killaire was overjoyed to finally have a part to play in far more than she would ever ask of a horse again. His day off had been more than earned.

Instead Lucinda rode a bright-eyed bouncing Killaire into the parade that preceded the show-jumping. Killaire, once declarations had closed, had stopped being worked seriously and was taken out each day for lively hacks. He had caught sight of the dreaded Serpent on one of these hacks, and his rider had quite a job dissuading him that he wasn't meant to jump it. Killaire was over-joyed to finally have a part to play in the proceedings, and wrinkled his lips in a happy smile as he jogged around the arena behind the Union Jack bearer, in company with Bleak Hills, Topper Too and Felday Farmer.

That afternoon the Canadians triumphantly held onto their convincing lead, but the American team could not fend off the Germans and they dropped back to third. They were recompensed by Bruce hanging onto his individual lead and clinching his second term of office. Runner up to Bruce was Irishman John Watson on Cambridge Blue, whose clear round in the show-jumping brought him up from sixth to second. Of the Brits, Richard moved up to fifth, and Jane and Topper to seventh, and Lizzie was the only other finisher in nineteenth place.

The 1978 World Championships hold mixed memories and emotions for many. It seemed that Lexington had been the right place, but at the wrong time of year.

7   A Change of Jockey

Two days after the Championship ended, Gossip and Killaire plus their friends flew back to England. Gossip's fighting spirit and strong constitution had ensured a rapid recovery. It was interesting to note that one of the official vets at Lexington, who checked all the heart rates of the competing horses before the competition began, was very impressed at the slow, strong beat of Gossip's. The average rate at rest is thirty-six beats per minute; Gossip's was twenty-eight – amazing for a horse who five years ago had failed the vet from a supposed heart problem.

Returning to a chilly England preparing for autumn, Gossip was turned out in the field for a long rest. Killaire remained in work and in mid-October competed at Boekelo, where he was fifth.

Another campaigner from Lexington joined Appleshaw that autumn, in the shape of a little grey horse called Bandolier, who had been ridden by Joanne Bridgeman for the New Zealand team. In accordance with OCL policy, Bandolier had his name changed. He became Mairangi Bay. His slight, part-Arab pony-bred looks belied his toughness and jumping ability, and his effortless movement. He had completed Lexington at the cost of two falls and a stop, but had managed to keep out of trouble at the Serpent and had collected only 28 time faults, proving he had speed. Joanne could not afford to fly Bandolier back to New Zealand and so, regretfully, she had to put him on the market along with the other Kiwis' horses. Lucinda had not registered much interest in the horse until Lady Hugh Russell commented that he might be her type.

The outcome was that Bandolier found a new home and a new name, and had to hastily grow a thicker coat for the

OP) Gossip's sire – Ardfert (taken 1976).
3OVE) Gossip at Goffs sales
llsbridge (August 1969).
GHT) Gossip as a foal with his
ther Jut Gold (1968). *George Manley*

(ABOVE) Showing confidence: Gossip and Katie's first event (March 1974).
(BELOW) Their first Tidworth: Gossip throws a massive leap over the Bourne crossing (May 1974).

(TOP) **His best test to date: Katie and Gossip at Burghley 1975.** *John Elliot*
(ABOVE) **A muddy Katie and Gossip on the cross country at Tidworth 1975, after their fall on the flat on phase A.** *Findlay Davidson*

(LEFT) Gossip making nothing of one of the Bughley fences (1975). *John Hughes*
(TOP) Dressage in Rehtein's saddle: Luhmühlen 1977. *E. Andersen*
(ABOVE) Representing England – Gossip springs off Fort Lexington (World
Championships 1978). *Milton C. Toby*

(ABOVE) Shelswell O.D.G. March 1980. Gossip shows rare acquiescence in the dressage. . . .
(RIGHT) but shows his all too frequent contrariness, this time in a disasterous test at Badminton 1981. *W. Capjon*
(BELOW) Foot perfect: Charlie and Gossip enter the Lake (Badminton 1980).
(BELOW RT) Showjumping into 7th place in the bitless bridle: The Alternate Olympics, Fontainebleau 1980.

(TOP) All is redeemed cross country: Gossip and Charlie over the Pardubice (Badminton 1981). *Ross Laney*
(ABOVE) On their way to a clear round. Gossip and Charlie in perfect harmony over the Keeper's rails (Badminton 1981). *Peter Ayres*

(ABOVE) Summer at grass at Appleshaw. *Alison Hicks*
(BELOW) A hideous sense of humour. Gossip has no inhibitions. (Rotherfield O.D.E. 1982). *Findlay Davidson*

encroaching northern hemisphere winter. He was to be OCL's little white hope for the future.

Charlie had been kept busy throughout the autumn running the yard and working the horses whilst Lucinda and Lisa were away. He did not ride in any three-day events but picked up several miles of experience on young horses in a number of one-day events.

By December Gossip had recovered all his condition and looked as strong and well as ever. His sense of humour had not diminished either.

One afternoon, Lisa went out to check on him and his companions, Be Fair and another advanced eventer, Discovery Bay. The field was empty. Then Lisa heard snorts from a neighbouring field. Puffing up to the top of a rise, Lisa saw Gossip leading his band along the headland. She ran back towards the house, jumped into her car and drove the two hundred yards along the road to the next house, parking her car across the driveway. As she stepped out, Gossip trotted round the corner, a jubilantly wicked smirk on his face, with his troops following obediently in the rear. He skidded to a halt as he almost collided with Lisa, and his mischievous expression switched to petulant disappointment when he saw he had been foiled. His troops feigned innocence of the entire escapade, as Lisa laughingly scolded them and put them back in their field.

Gossip never forgot the fun and havoc caused by changing fields, and on another day he popped out of his field and cantered up and down the jumping lane that ran alongside the outdoor school, knowing his actions would upset the horse Lucinda was trying to school. Concentration successfully diverted, Gossip kept up this game whilst Lucinda sat and watched, giggling helplessly.

In the second week of 1979, Gossip started work again in preparation for Badminton, as did Killaire.

But it wasn't until Gossip began faster work that Lucinda realised Lexington had left its mark. Firstly his wind wasn't so clear; he began to puff on his work-outs, something he had never done before, and his wind was never to be as good again.

A check on his heart rate revealed that although it was in good working order, its resting rate would never be as low as twenty-eight beats per minute.

Consequently Lucinda found that she could work him more conventionally. He still fought every stride but was not quite so impetuously wild. Lucinda formulated a proper interval-training programme for him, determined to have him super-fit for Badminton. She feared that if he became tired he would remember those last fences at Lexington and how much they had cost him; she didn't want him to become disheartened.

At the beginning of March, Gossip won the open class at an indoor jumping show at Wylye. At the end of the month, he competed at Rushall, where, due to the differing opinions between horse and rider in the dressage, Gossip finished only sixth. Paradoxically, after the previous year's anxieties over having to ride him with no control, Lucinda now found him too rideable. She worried that he wasn't truly on form, although apart from his tractability across country, there was no other reason to suppose he wasn't as well as ever.

Killaire, on the other hand, was feeling and looking magnificent, and hared round the Rushall cross-country course at such a rate he finished with the same amount of time faults as Gossip, and his better dressage put him third. He did cause a minor panic at the end of the cross country, when he pulled up with blood pouring down one front leg. A vet, hastily summoned, stemmed the bleeding and discovered a small puncture wound behind Killaire's elbow. Killaire, it seemed, had tucked his front feet up so high over one fence, that the small stud in his front shoe had stabbed into him. Luckily, the injury was not serious.

Brigstock was to be the next competition, but at 7 am on the morning of the trials, the organisers very sadly and reluctantly had to cancel the event. A night-long deluge had submerged the horsebox park under several inches of water, and the going on the cross country was soft, wet and spongey.

So Rushall had to suffice as the only pre-Badminton warm-up, and in mid-April, Lucinda, Gossip and Killaire, along with 'nannies' Lisa and Liz, set out for the familiar parkland in Gloucestershire.

After the dressage phase, Killaire chalked up an eye-rubbing score of 49.4, and he stood second to Judy Bradwell's Castlewellan. Lucinda appreciatively contributed his good mark to the combined teachings of David Hunt and team trainer Ernst Bachinger, plus help from Brigid Maxwell who had worked under Herbert Rehbein for five years. Between them they had encouraged maximum use of Killaire's short stride, and brought flair and sparkle to his paces, which, when added to accurate movements, had produced a delightful test.

Gossip was not so generously received. After a test that Lucinda felt was one of their better efforts, Gossip's mark score was 72. Lucinda gloomily reflected that the judges were beginning to mark Gossip down before he had even set foot in the arena, knowing only too well what the next seven minutes would bring.

Once again Gossip was first to go on phase A. On phase B Gossip showed he was not his usual self by finishing the steeplechase only seven seconds inside the time, instead of his usual thirty.

Out on the cross country he galloped as fast as ever between fences, but his jump did not engender in Lucinda quite the thrill it had a year ago. But, for his single error on the course, Lucinda blames herself.

Galloping down from the Park Wall jump, they approached the Footbridge, a fence design Frank Weldon had stolen from Lexington and which had three alternative routes. On the right was a set of rails with a bounce distance over a ditch; on the left was a ditch and bounce to a parallel. The centre route required a massive leap over an angled bridge across the ditch, and if riders didn't take off from the correct spot at the correct speed they would be in trouble.

Lucinda opted for the left-hand route. As they neared the fence, Lucinda steadied Gossip to what she thought was the best speed for their line. Gossip had his eyes firmly fixed on the parallel. It suddenly dawned on Lucinda that she hadn't made allowances for the fact that Gossip wouldn't sight the ditch until the last minute. Gossip, taken completely by surprise at the ground disappearing in front of him, piled over the ditch and slammed up against the parallel, unable to

organise his legs in time to take off. Lucinda quickly turned
Gossip and jumped over an easy escape route that she had
spotted when walking the course, and headed for the next
fence. But her suspicions aroused on the steeplechase were
being unhappily confirmed. Gossip was not really enjoying
himself. Kicking him on through the Luckington Lane
complex, he felt dull and leaden, and over the last few drops
he stumbled and pecked, unable to make the effort to hold
himself up.

A very depressed jockey followed Lisa and Gossip back to
the stables, where an eager Killaire was waiting his turn.
Lucinda slumped down on the ramp of the lorry, all
enthusiasm doused by the knowledge that she was actually
tired from riding Gossip round a course. What had Lexington
done to the bravest, toughest horse she had ever known? The
inspiration she needed to ride Killaire was swamped in a mire
of despair.

Lucinda's family, Lisa and Liz, forced optimistic encouragement. They reminded Lucinda of Killaire's past brilliant
performances, particularly over the huge course at Ledyard.
Temporarily refuelled, Lucinda squeezed Killaire round the
steeplechase, finishing just within the permitted five minutes.
But by the time Lucinda had reached the Box at the end of
phase C, all her attacking spirit had dissipated under a cloud
of depression.

Ten minutes later Killaire surged out of the start of phase
D, his rider bristling with determination and vigour. In those
few moments Pat Burgess, who has helped Lucinda so much
over the years, said a few words to her that sent jangling
messages along Lucinda's nerves. Lady Doreen added another
positive spur, 'Forget Lexington, you owe this to Killaire.' A
last-second reassurance from Lisa, 'He *can* do it. Don't forget
Ledyard,' shot home the adrenalin into brain and muscle.

Killaire jumped and galloped like he had never done before,
straight into the lead.

On Sunday, Gossip, who had collected no time penalties
despite his stop, was in eighth place. He had a rail down in the
show-jumping, but the happy disposition that he displayed
was all that Lucinda was concerned about, and he managed to

retain his position. Killaire had to go clear to win, and so far that day only three horses had achieved clear rounds.

Killaire made it four, and presented his rapturous owner, Charles Cyzer, with the Whitbread Trophy.

After Badminton, Lucinda decided to give Gossip the rest of the year off and not aim him for any three-day event that autumn. He had been 101 per cent fit for Badminton but Lexington had taxed his stamina more than anyone realised, and his body was not yet ready to absorb the punishing speed he inflicted on himself, nor were his muscles back to their full iron-tough strength. He was eleven years old and in his prime for a top-class eventer. With sensible programming, Gossip could have another two or three years at the top, but if Lucinda plugged on with him whilst memories of Lexington haunted their minds, Gossip's career would be over in months. Until Gossip felt his old self, there was no enjoyment for either of them in doing battle at three-day events. So, for the rest of 1979, Killaire wholly assumed the mantle of number one.

Meanwhile there was still the rest of the spring season to finish. Mairangi Bay, it seemed, also had some latent Lexington dust to shake off. He had finished third in the open class at Shelswell one-day event but had lacked the sparkle Lucinda wanted and enjoyed in her horses. Appreciating that he also had to cope with the climatic differences of the northern hemisphere, Lucinda allowed him an easy spring and a summer holiday with the benefit of the fresh spring grass.

In the third week of May, Lucinda, Charlie and Lisa crossed the Irish sea for the Punchestown three-day event. Lucinda was riding the seven-year-old Botany Bay, whom she had owned since he was three. Charlie's partner for his second-ever three-day event was Discovery Bay who, as Scimitar, was owned by Gill Suttle but had been leased to OCL, thus necessitating a change of name.

Sadly, Punchestown was a non-event for Charlie, as Discovery Bay ran a high temperature soon after arriving at the racecourse stabling. He had contracted a travel virus and had to be withdrawn. But Botany Bay more than made up for his friend's sickness by finishing second in the competition to Castlewellan and Judy Bradwell.

Then, in July, Charlie had an opportunity to ride Gossip.

Lucinda, although technically resting Gossip, knew that he would not revel in sitting in the field for the rest of the year. His mind was too active to remain in a state of hibernation for months on end. Apart from which, Lucinda did not want to let his muscles become completely soft, which meant he would take even longer to return to prime condition.

So to keep Gossip tuned and mentally alert without overtaxing him, Charlie and Gossip went show-jumping. They competed in several Foxhunter classes, including one at Hickstead, and won a class at a Windsor Park Equestrian Club show. Charlie put their success down to Gossip's ability to stop and turn on a sixpence and his instant acceleration.

Lucinda had also won a Foxhunter on Gossip in the spring, and decided to ride him in the regional final at a big show in Somerset. Lucinda and Gossip both gulped when they saw the course, and he did well to have only two fences down and a foot in the water. Lucinda's over-riding memory of that day, though, is that Gossip felt tired at the end. The previous day she had given him a forty-minute school, and it seemed to have taken the edge off him. A year ago, it would have been inconceivable that Gossip should feel jaded after so little work. It reinforced her decision not to event him too soon.

While Charlie had fun with Gossip, Killaire was manfully holding Lucinda's place in the British team for the fifth year in succession. This year it was for the European Championships at Luhmühlen in early September.

In Germany, Killaire produced a superb test, surpassing even his Badminton performance. On the cross country, which contained almost fifty individual jumping efforts (ten more than at Lexington), he gave Lucinda one of the most confident rides ever, and finished fourth fastest of the day. He took the British team into an enormous lead from the Irish, and placed himself third individually.

His magnificent, selfless achievement had been in vain. On Saturday evening he was lame and despite concerted efforts by Peter Scott-Dunn, Lucinda and Liz, nothing alleviated the problem. There was no obvious symptom to indicate whether the soreness was in the muscle, foot or tendon, but the sad fact remained: he could not show-jump the next day. His withdrawal helped the Irish, Killaire's home side, to the winner's rostrum. Maybe it could be said he helped his country after all.

The weekend immediately following Luhmühlen, Charlie and Discovery Bay became the centre of attention, when Charlie contested Burghley. Lucinda did not have a ride, feeling Burghley was a little too advanced for Botany Bay, but she was there on foot to give Charlie moral support.

Discovery Bay was a powerfully built horse, kind natured but with a neurotic, highly strung temperament that took firm patience to understand and control. He performed a passable dressage test and went on to give Charlie a wonderful, memorable ride across country. However, due to a slight mishap at the sunken wall, Charlie somehow lost his two false front teeth (the originals had been knocked out in a racing fall) in Discovery Bay's mane, and finished the course sporting a toothless grin.

Discovery Bay went clear in the show-jumping on Sunday and although not finishing amongst the placings Charlie was thrilled with the result.

At the beginning of October, Lucinda and Gossip competed at Batsford one-day event. Principally, Lucinda wanted to see how he felt and test his reaction to a cross-country course; she also hoped it would whet his appetite for competition in 1980.

Her conclusions after the event were happy ones. Gossip finished second in his section and felt as powerful and strong as ever, revelling in being allowed to gallop and jump at speed again. Moreover, he showed he was a more mature Gossip, no longer the reckless hoyden but a seasoned event horse who had confidence in his abilities and the *joie de vivre* to produce a sparkling, exhilarating peformance.

In January 1980, Lucinda spent three weeks in Germany with two of her younger horses at Herbert Rehbein's, absorbing as much as possible of the intrinsic mysteries of dressage, and hoping an answer might materialise that would lead her to the enlightenment of Gossip.

Back in England in February, a new working pupil arrived at Appleshaw with his horse. Their journey had taken over three days to complete and spanned more than 12,000 miles. Australian rider David Green and his ex-rodeo horse, Swift Deal, were to attempt Badminton for the first time, and Lucinda had agreed that they could use Appleshaw as a base for their preparation.

Lucinda had entered Gossip, Killaire, who was now sound, and Mairangi for the Whitbread Championships, but under the rules she would only be permitted to ride two of her entries.

Six weeks before Badminton, Lucinda casually asked Charlie whether he would prefer to ride Killaire or Gossip at Badminton. When Charlie had regained his senses, his answer was prompt. Charlie always favoured the under-dog, and Gossip, with his unpredictability in the dressage, was a horse that could come from behind. Gossip was also his type of horse and they had begun to forge a fluent partnership during the previous autumn's show-jumping.

A technical hitch immediately presented itself, when it became apparent that Charlie had not yet gained the qualifications to ride at Badminton. So Lucinda had to request special dispensation from the powers that be, for Charlie to have permission to ride, and which was granted.

Charlie wasted no time and began riding Gossip seriously from that day on, realising every second spent in the saddle was precious if they were not to disgrace themselves at Badminton.

A cross-country school was high on the list of priorities, and Charlie took Gossip down to Wylye for a session with Lady Hugh. One fence on the course that Lady Hugh had plotted for Charlie, was a wide, solid sleeper table. 'Don't worry, Charlie,' said Lucinda, who had come down to watch. 'One thing Gossip won't do is stand off. He'll just gallop on, shuffle in a stride and pop over.'

Gossip galloped up to the table at his usual cracking pace, stood off a stride, and made complete fools of them both.

With Gossip's fast work, Charlie's experience with flighty, runaway racehorses gave him an advantage when galloping Gossip. 'Once you found the right wavelength, you were away,' remembers Charlie, 'but if you chose to fight, you were lost.' The secret lay in always being willing to reach a compromise. It was never, ever a case of using brute strength, ordering Gossip to do this or that. Every command had to be preceded by 'Please'. The knack with Gossip was to be a strong rider, without him knowing.

But dressage was another language. To Charlie, dressage was a series of indistinct patterns that had yet to really form into any concrete solidity of shape and direction. In this sphere, Charlie was still very much at sea and more than a little confused.

Charlie rode Gossip at Shelswell and Rushall one-day events that spring. On advice from Lucinda, Charlie rode strongly through the wet, holding conditions of Rushall, and they finished with the fastest time. None of the fences at either course had presented any problems to the new partnership, and Charlie was by now well adapted to Gossip's individual style.

So it was that three confident riders, their grooms and four horses left for Badminton in the middle of April.

The almost reverential atmosphere of Badminton was so utterly different to anything Charlie had encountered before that he was undaunted by the challenge that lay ahead. He seemed blissfully unaware of the pressures that could be exerted on the better-known riders and was far more concerned with the practicalities of locating Gossip's stable and his own accommodation, and whether he got lost between the two.

The course was naturally the focal point for all the riders and Charlie fully respected the formidable fences that dotted the park. However, he had tremendous confidence in Lucinda's horses and especially in Gossip. He was sure enough of their partnership to know that, provided the wavelength stayed clear, Gossip would jump whatever Charlie put him at, such was the horse's astonishing athleticism.

Charlie's most worrying problem was remembering which

line to take into each fence. He had the utmost regard for Lucinda's expertise in walking and riding a course. Knowing Gossip as well as she did, Lucinda was able to pick out the most suitable routes for Charlie to take, and Charlie trusted her advice implicitly.

He hoped his confessed lousy memory would not let him down, and that he would remember which post in the fence-line or which tree in the distance he was supposed to line up with as he galloped into each jump. Would he remember whether he had to hold for two short strides, or kick on for a long one in the combinations? And he had to be well acquainted with the easier, slow routes at fences in case things did not go according to plan.

Lucinda also reminded Charlie that the huge crowds pressing round the ropes at each fence, could blot out a piece of vegetation marking a line into a fence, and that a bristly patch of undergrowth could disappear completely under the tramp of many feet. There was a lot to think about.

Charlie does not recollect any major horrors during Gossip's dressage test that Badminton, and their mark of 72.8 certainly indicates that it was neither 'fair nor foul'.

On cross-country day Charlie was worried. Not about the course or the milling spectators, but whether he and Gossip would arrive at the start of each phase at the correct time because Gossip was napping as much as ever.

They sped round the first two phases without problems, Gossip finishing the steeplechase inside the time and still full of running. Then on phase C they amassed an extraordinary 18 time penalties. Charlie later admitted that a call of nature was the reason for the baffling time faults. What Gossip must have thought as Charlie disappeared behind a tree . . .

On phase D, any misgivings Lucinda might have had about allowing Charlie to ride Gossip, vanished at the same speed with which Gossip and Charlie attacked the fences. Badminton 1980 will be remembered as a tough course, emphasised by the unusually hard ground for the time of year, which caused a lot of horses to become footsore. But for Gossip, the going acted as a springboard. He was at his best on firm ground and his confidence mounted as he and Charlie raced away from each fence. An enormous leap at the Vicarage Vee requested by Charlie, brought gasps to his supporters as they watched on the close-circuit TV in the Box. But Gossip soared through the air, in tune with Charlie's wishes, and landed well clear.

It was only at the end of the course that they made their first and last mistake. Or rather Charlie did, and very much in the same vein that Katie had done in the show-jumping at Burghley.

They were three fences from home and still clear. 'My God,' thought Charlie, 'we are nearly there.' He relaxed as Gossip jumped over the first part of the bounce in Huntsman's Close. As Charlie folded forward, anticipating Gossip's take-off over the second part, he made the classical mistake of being fractionally in front of the movement. Gossip jammed to a halt.

'Lesson learnt,' thought Charlie ruefully, as he rectified the error, and they galloped towards the final fence, Whitbread Bar, and the finish.

Only three horses came through without time or jump penalties and Gossip had yet again defied the odds and the clock, despite his stop. Lucinda had endured an unhappy time with Mairangi, who had pulled up lame after the steeplechase and had been retired. Killaire, who never performed at anything less than his best, scampered round with only a handful of time faults, and was lying second behind Helen Butler on Merganser, with New Zealander Mark Todd on Southern Comfort third, and Ultimus, ridden by the Swede Goran Breisner, lying fourth. Gossip had cleverly manoeuvred himself into eleventh place, much to a delighted Charlie's surprise.

The other withdrawal in the Appleshaw contingent was David's Swift Deal, who had not been started on phase A. Swift had bruised his leg in the field a few weeks earlier, and although he was sound, it was deemed wiser not to run him on the hard ground and risk jarring the leg again.

On Sunday afternoon the crowds were kept on the edge of their seats in the show-jumping phase. Clear rounds were infrequent but Ultimus and Southern Comfort both achieved them, putting pressure on the leaders. Killaire brought howls of dismay when he put a foot in the water. Then poor Helen suffered the agonising humiliation of lowering four rails, which caused her to slide to fourth place. Her demise shot Southern Comfort into the lead above Killaire and let Ultimus into third. A jubilant Mark Todd became the first Kiwi to receive the Whitbread Trophy.

Gossip kept his eleventh place, even though he had a rail down, and kept Charlie in the front row of prize-winners. It was a meteoric achievement for someone who had never ridden in a three-day event two years ago.

8 Back in Power

The British team selectors were not only impressed with Gossip's obvious return to top form, but also with his latest jockey. They put both Killaire and Gossip on the short-list for the Alternative Olympics at Fontainebleau in France, which were to be held in the third week of August. The agreement between the selectors and Lucinda and Charlie was, that if both horses were needed to make up the six allowed to participate in France, then Charlie would ride Gossip. But if for some reason Killaire fell by the wayside, then Lucinda would take the ride on Gossip.

In fact it looked doubtful that Charlie would have a ride, as there were considerably more experienced riders on the short-list, but Charlie considered it quite amazing that the selectors had even nominated him.

Lucinda rode both horses at the only selection trial at Dauntsey on August 3rd, and Killaire and Gossip showed they were still in good form. Twelve days later came the final trot up at Wylye, before Peter Scott-Dunn, chef d'équipe Major Malcolm Wallace and the selectors. Sadly Killaire was lame. Earlier in the month, he had put a hind leg through his stable wall at Appleshaw, when he had become cast one evening. Initially, it seemed he had sustained only slight bruising to his hock and all looked well after a few days' rest. But some recent fast work had brought the soreness back, and Peter diagnosed a bruised Achilles' tendon.

So after two years in the wilderness, Gossip found himself once again in the fore.

The journey out to Fontainebleau was beset by travel problems. In France commercial fishermen were waging a large-scale industrial dispute. Consequently, most of the seaports open to cross-channel ferries were being blockaded. Malcolm was becoming worried, wondering how best to transport his team across. The horses were due to leave on the Sunday before the competition began. The option of crossing to a Belgian port and then driving across to France was not favoured because of the many hours the horses would have to spend on the road, and the risk of delays at the border between Belgium and France. Even without hold-ups, the horses would have very little time to recover from their trip before being thrust into a major competition.

Malcolm decided to have the horses flown out and a small plane was made available at Southampton Airport on the Monday before the event began. There was only enough room on board for six horses and twelve people, whose number included Lisa, one of the three grooms to fly with the horses. The trunks of tack, luggage and horse-feed had to go by road, as did the other three grooms and all the riders, taking the long circuitous route through Belgium.

It was a very relieved chef d'équipe that finally found his troops, all safely in one piece, in the sanded woods outside the town of Fontainebleau.

The riders were accommodated in nearby hotels, but Lisa and the other grooms had to laugh when they saw their campsite for the week. As Lisa wrote in an article later, 'The entire set-up reminded us of the TV programme M. A. S. H.' Their sleeping quarters were canvas army tents, showering facilities were non-existent as was any hot water, and loos were in very short supply.

The horses were installed in temporary stables close by. Gossip was unruffled by the short flight, a mere trifle compared to his international jet-setting to America. He was in terrific form and made his presence clearly known by testing the walls of his stable with his heels. He only desisted when Lisa waved his hobbles threateningly at him.

Lucinda, still at loggerheads over his dressage, was determined to have Gossip subdued for his test, which was scheduled for Friday morning. On Thursday she took him for an energetic ride, encompassing all of phases A and C, a distance of some ten miles plus, at a bone-rattling trot, in the hopes the exercise might take the edge off him. Gossip wore a bitless bridle to preserve his mouth for Saturday, which gave him even more excuse to steam off at his own pace.

On Friday morning Lisa had a terrible fright when her alarm failed to go off and she overslept. Other grooms rushed to her rescue. Whilst two people plaited Gossip's mane and another brushed off the shavings, Lisa tacked him up. Gossip was so amazed at the sudden surge of people around him, he forgot to fidget and kick as he usually did when being groomed.

Thanks to all her helpers, Lisa had Gossip polished and spruce by the time Lucinda wanted to ride him.

Ernst Bachinger was once again helping the team, and again he agreed not to interfere with Gossip, knowing the results would be, if anything, negative. He stood, watching from the collecting ring, as Lucinda worked Gossip before his test.

As Lucinda trotted round, she suddenly had a mental blank over whether there were five or six steps in the rein-back movement in the test. She pulled up beside Ernst to ask him. 'Wiz Gossip it doesn't really matter, does it?' intoned the Austrian, wryly amused at the difference it might make to Gossip's marks. Lucinda could hardly stop laughing.

Lisa led Gossip as near as she was allowed to the dressage arena. He was so full of high spirits he was napping and refusing to walk in any definite direction. He then proceeded to frolic through the test, whilst Lucinda sat in silence, knowing that any interference on her part would wind up the tension. Ironically the only movement he performed with some semblance of discipline was the rein-back. Otherwise, he lived up to his old nick-name and goosed his neck, hollowed his back and turned his test into a joke. After the final halt and salute at X, he swaggered out of the arena, defiantly unconcerned that his mark of 83 had placed him fourth from bottom.

The cross country was long and twisty with many fences at maximum height and spread. Several jumps came only a few strides off a turn, making them ride bigger than they actually were. The many twists and turns over the undulating course would tire a horse quickly. Fitness would be at a premium.

For the first three phases, Lucinda decided to use the bitless bridle, which was fitted over Gossip's snaffle bridle. This meant that on phases A and C she could ride him with the former, preserving his mouth to the last possible minute, then, apart from on the steeplechase, the only real pressure on his mouth would come from the cross-country phase, before which the bitless bridle would be removed altogether.

He napped at the start of phase A after the countdown had ended, so Lisa could only watch helplessly as Gossip spun round on his hind legs, refusing to go forwards, exactly as Be Fair had done five years before in Luhmühlen.

At last Lucinda succeeded in persuading him onto the track of phase A, down which he tanked relentlessly. He easily made the steeplechase time on phase B, and charged off down phase C on the six-odd miles to the Box.

Refreshed in the Box by Lisa, and with the bitless bridle now removed, he was led to the start of phase D.

'*Allez vite*' was obviously Gossip's foremost thought, as he shot out of the start box and over the first fence. The second jump, Napoleon's Hat, consisted of a steep bank up to a log, and an equally precipitous slope down the other side. Gossip rocketed up the bank and over the log. His impetuous dash landed him halfway down the slope on the far side. This rather reckless attack, which was very 'un-Gossip', shook him considerably and he was almost hesitant in front of the next fence, a straightforward parallel filled in with gorse.

Thereafter his confidence returned and he gave Lucinda a stunning ride, surpassing even his performance at Lexington. Fontainebleau was a true championship course and the short approaches to some fences really put horses to the test.

Gossip felt wonderfully strong and powerful, right to the finish. Any vestiges of memories of Lexington had been flung off. Gossip was back to his old self.

Sadly the rest of the Brits did not fare so well. Individuals Mark Phillips and Lincoln had been withdrawn after the dressage, as Mark was not happy with the horse's soundness. The other 'loner', Rachel Bayliss on her young but highly talented Mystic Minstrel, led after the dressage phase but crashed out with two falls on the cross country.

Of the team members, Chris Collins on Gamble had a heavy fall, leaving Chris slightly concussed and causing his retirement. Kilcashel, mount of Richard Meade, had not even reached the cross country: he had contracted azoturia, a form of muscle cramp, on phase C. Merganser and Helen Butler had escaped with just one refusal at the water, so only he and Gossip were able to make it through to Sunday's show-jumping.

After the cross country, Gossip had climbed to tenth place, and a clear in the show-jumping moved him up a few rungs higher to seventh. A report in *Horse and Hound* by Frank Weldon commented that Gossip's ascent of fifty-eight places after the dressage must be something of a world record.

On the Sunday of Fontainebleau, Lucinda purchased a horse. This horse's dressage was nearly as bad as Gossip's and Lucinda showed no interest in him until David Green, who was becoming more than a working pupil, told her how well he had seen the horse perform a cross country in Australia. So Lucinda agreed to try the horse out. Her breath was taken away by the little horse's kangaroo-like ability over a fence and the unconventional way he galloped off, so like Gossip. The little Aussie newcomer to Appleshaw was called Regal Realm.

Back from France, this time evading the blockade and returning by ferry, Gossip settled into his autumnal sojourn in the field. Lucinda headed for Burghley, with Charlie and Discovery Bay, on a comparatively new horse, Foxy Bubble.

Foxy, a nine-year-old, 16.3 hh, bright bay gelding, was then owned by the British Equestrian Federation. He had completed half of Badminton that year with Jane Holderness-Roddam, but Jane had retired him at the lake, feeling Foxy had mentally coped with as much as he could. After Badminton, Jane wanted to take a temporary break from eventing, so Lucinda was offered the ride.

Foxy was the kindest, friendliest horse one could wish to meet. But he was also rather dotty and found it hard work co-ordinating his brain and limbs. His breeder, Col. Cookson, had written to Lucinda describing how he used to watch the gangly young Foxy hurtling around the paddocks and falling over his own legs. Col. Cookson was quite surprised that Foxy never ended up breaking his own neck.

He was also a very spooky horse. Lucinda was cantering round Toby Balding's circular tan track one summer's day when a clump of dandelions suddenly waved to Foxy in the breeze. Foxy stopped as though he had smacked into a wall, and Lucinda flew straight over his head, totally unprepared for his sudden jamming on of the brakes.

Another time, Australian friend and top dressage rider, Ron Patterson, was schooling Foxy at Appleshaw. 'Don't see what you are all complaining about,' he said as he worked Foxy, the horse moving forward smoothly and calmly, all concentration on Ron. In the next moment Ron found himself pitched forward abruptly onto Foxy's neck, his mouth full of mane. Foxy had spied Lucinda pulling her sweater off over her head and had screeched to a halt at this headless phenomenon.

But it was pigs that really freaked Foxy. On a hot day in July, Lucinda was hacking Foxy along a quiet road. She turned up a track alongside a field which contained what looked like mounds of hay. As Foxy passed by, the 'mounds', which turned out to be little brown piglets, leapt up and ran away squealing. Foxy flipped and reversed down to the road as fast as his legs could carry him. Nothing Lucinda did would persuade him to go back up the track. From that day on, any pig or suspicious-looking mound caused Foxy to flee, and nothing would induce him to go past it.

Lucinda had had Foxy for only a few weeks before Burghley, and was finding him a very different ride to the compact, fiery Gossip. Foxy was an extremely elegant horse but was also far harder to hold together, and needed a strong pair of legs from the rider to maintain and compound his power and impulsion. She had ridden Foxy round the Midland Bank one-day event championships at Locko in August, when a fairly haphazard ride on this strong gawky horse had resulted to two stops, and near misses as Foxy inadvertently clouted fences with his dangling legs, attention fixed elsewhere.

So it was with deep misgivings that Lucinda and Foxy lolloped off down to the first of the Burghley fences on cross-country day. His good dressage marks were chiefly due to his impressive movement rather than accuracy in the test, during which he had spooked at any and every opportunity, his mind far away.

In the vague hope that she might hold him together more effectively, Lucinda decided to use a double bridle for all three parts of the event. To her relief, the new brakes on the cross country worked, and Foxy made a very professional job of the course and finished with a clear round. After the show-jumping phase, he ended the competition in ninth place.

Unhappily, Charlie had a less successful time. Discovery Bay made a bad jump over the fence in the wood before the Lower Trout Hatchery. Charlie was in two minds whether to continue as he wasn't sure the horse was feeling right. He decided to jump the next, but Discovery Bay, very unusually, hit the rail hard, and came down the other side. Charlie remembers crawling frantically away from Discovery Bay on hands and knees to avoid being squashed. Charlie then retired and led Discovery Bay back to the stables. Later, it was apparent the horse had strained a tendon.

9 New Scene, Old Faces

As the autumn months of 1980 slid by, there were changes at Appleshaw and I found myself back in charge of operations, but with only Gossip's wicked face to remind me of the old days. My chestnut hero, Be Fair, was no more. He had irreparably damaged a tendon in the hunting field and was now watching us from above, as was Lucinda's father, the General, whose kindly wisdom and advice I badly missed.

Gossip was now firmly ensconced at Appleshaw, secure and happy that this was really home. His genuine fear and mistrust had disappeared, but he was still suspicious of strangers, particularly men. New girls, working in the yard, were tested out by Gossip. On their initial introduction to him, he would park his bottom by the door and snake his head round, ears back, daring them to enter his stable. If they backed off and left him, Gossip was delighted and carried on his fearsome charade for as long as he could, until the girls grew wise to his trickery.

One trainee who joined us for a year, absolutely refused to go into Gossip's stable. I tried to help her overcome her fears and explain that he didn't really mean what he implied. Six months later I noticed she had plucked up the courage to skep out his stable. Then, a few weeks after that, I came out of the tackroom one morning, armed with boots and a New Zealand rug for Gossip, who was to be turned out in the field. Across the yard, I saw her beaming face looking out of Gossip's door. 'He's all ready,' she said, unable to stop grinning. 'You mean you've put Gossip's boots on?' I gabbled, staring at her in amazement and dropping the armful I was carrying. 'Yes, and his New Zealand,' she said proudly. I don't know who was more stunned, Gossip or myself. Gossip was furious and went into a big sulk. He had so enjoyed having someone to bait over the past months; Susan had been his most successful victim.

Gossip had even less success with the next trainee, Michelle, who very quickly saw through his disguise. Gossip felt quite cheated.

Lucinda and Charlie both spent November and December in the warmer climes of Australia. Lucinda had been invited to compete in the Melbourne three-day event on two generously loaned horses, and was planning to visit the Green family, David having returned home after Fontainebleau. Charlie was to combine a holiday with teaching at a series of clinics.

I spent the quiet autumn days tidying and organising for the coming spring season, and making friends with the new equine faces at Appleshaw.

The most recent arrival was Ponch (Regal Realm) and he quickly staked a claim for my affections. Ponch was very nervous and the slightest noise startled him, but he had a gentle temperament combined with a certain aloofness. At first impression he seemed a rather boring horse, which he most certainly was not. His intelligence out-ranked even that of Gossip and Be Fair, and he had a far more adult manner than either. Whilst Gossip would revert to his napping, and Be Fair would occasionally give vent to his red-headed temper, Ponch never lapsed to any such display. He was a very superior person but without being in any way pompous. The only time he let himself go was when he was on holiday out at grass. Then he became as though wild, not in temperament, but as if he had never been handled by humans. He became impossible to catch and the only way he would let anyone come close was if they had no rope or halter in their hands. Perhaps he likened it to being back on the vast desolate acres of his native Australia, where his life had begun.

While everyone was away Ponch gave me and Lucy, who was helping, a dreadful fright by contracting a strange virus that caused his legs, belly and sheath area to swell to an enormous size, as did the glands under his throat. His temperature soared and his skin was covered in spots. The symptoms had the appearance of an allergy. Various injections administered by Paul Farrington, our vet, reduced the swelling and Ponch stopped looking like a baby elephant. But he had lost all the condition he had struggled to gain in adapting to life in the northern hemisphere. I prayed Ponch would not produce any more bizarre horrors before Lucinda returned. Her supposed 'rising-star' now looked incapable of trotting round a Pony Club course, such was his state of health.

The little grey Kiwi, Mairangi, also had a kindly temperament, and a touch of cheek that made him that bit special. He had spent the rest of 1980 in the field, recovering from his leg injury sustained at Badminton, and was now sound and ready for 1981.

There was also another grey face I had to meet, a very innocent-looking one, prettily put together like a Welsh mountain pony's. It belonged to Leadhills, who competed under the OCL name of Beagle Bay. 'Biggles' as he was often nick-named, had an expression of 'sweetness and light' – but he could be so naughty. He kicked in a far more lethal fashion than Gossip when being groomed, but again, not from ill-humour, he was just ticklish. He didn't walk down the road, he bounced, with ears tightly pricked, poking out from a fluffy white mass of forelock. He would shy and spin away from a suspicious object before the rider realised what was happening, and, when he was feeling like it, could deposit anyone on the ground with one lightning corkscrew buck. He was an advanced eventer and Lucinda had come third with him at the Wylye three-day event in the autumn of 1979. He had then been given a year off, having sprained a tendon, but now, like Mairangi, was sound and ready for work.

The other horses were Foxy Bubble, Botany Bay, and two or three young horses, including an irrepressibly naughty three-year-old called Moreton Bay, whose name was to be changed in later years to Brass Monkey.

By the New Year Lucinda and Charlie had returned from Australia sporting healthy tans, making us feel even colder and paler.

Badminton, as always, was the fulcrum around which the spring events were organised. Charlie, who had been such a success with Gossip the previous spring, was given another opportunity to ride him again at Badminton. Lucinda was aiming to take Mairangi and Killaire, now completely sound after a long rest at his home in Sussex.

To Gossip's horror, he was obliged to endure a series of dressage lessons that spring with Charlie, under the critical eye of David Hunt. Charlie, who openly admitted he hadn't the experience to ride a horse like Gossip in a dressage arena, spent the best part of each lesson on his feet watching David ride him. David, through his brilliant and technically correct riding, soon had a grudging and still slightly ungiving Gossip powering round the school like a Rolls Royce. Within five minutes of Charlie mounting him, Gossip would revert to his staccato self, sensing the subtle change of authority. In one lesson, Charlie and David rode Gossip four or five times each. Every time David rode him, Gossip made dressage look like simplicity itself. But when they swapped, Gossip switched in minutes to being 'Gossip'. Gossip's change of attitude according to the rider was fascinating in its suddenness.

However, the gap between Charlie's and David's techniques did close a little by March. The first event was Shelswell, and Charlie succeeded in working Gossip until he had him as nearly 'on the bit' as he could hope, although Gossip was, as ever, showing his usual signs of resistance. Charlie kept a short rein contact until after the test, for fear that he would lose his link if he let him have a free rein beforehand. The ruse worked and Gossip performed a surprisingly normal test, giving Charlie optimism for the rest of the season.

But the rest of Gossip's challenge at Shelswell ended in the show-jumping. The going was sticky and holding, as it dried out from recent heavy rain, and Charlie could feel Gossip struggling to clear the fences. In the middle of the combination, Gossip ground to a halt, his neat little feet glued up to the fetlocks in mud. Charlie reckoned there would be no enjoyment for them on the cross country, and withdrew.

Annoyingly, the ground at the next event, Brigstock, was no better. Needing a run before Badminton, Charlie and Gossip set out on the cross country, but the mud sucked at the horses' legs and claimed Gossip as one of its victims when he and Charlie fell at a big parallel. This didn't unnerve Charlie because he realised their fall was partly his fault as he had ridden Gossip on a bad approach to the fence. But when Gossip nearly fell again, at the second last, Charlie was worried, thinking Gossip should have been sharpened up by the fall. He concluded that the clay-like ground could take some of the blame, gripping at Gossip's feet as he took off, causing him to lose his balance.

Lucinda had run Killaire and Mairangi at both events, and she was especially pleased with the little grey, who seemed happy in his work for the first time since she had bought him. Aside from his leg problems, Mairangi had constantly lacked sparkle in his attitude to life, and had plagued Lucinda with worry that he might have a blood disorder or some underlying affliction. Tests had revealed nothing significant, either internally or externally, and Mairangi remained a puzzle. But this spring he appeared brighter in his outlook, and Lucinda hoped he would keep up this frame of mind through Badminton. Killaire was bursting with his usual buoyant spirits, but Lucinda had made up her mind to let this be his last Badminton. Although he was only thirteen, Killaire was never designed to be an international event horse. He had a heart that would never say no, but Lucinda knew it was fairer to retire him before his body failed to measure up to his will.

As March turned to April the predicted showers held off and the ground began to dry out. By Badminton it was firm enough for Charlie to stop worrying how Gossip would cope. But he had mixed feelings about the dressage. David Hunt had brought Charlie and Gossip into greater harmony with each other, but Charlie was very aware that he still had a lot of catching-up to do in the knowledge of how to ride Gossip.

Gossip's test was on Thursday afternoon. In the morning David gave Charlie a lesson and Gossip worked exceptionally well. Hopes of a successful afternoon ran promisingly high.

But, true to form, a fickle Gossip confounded everyone's aspirations. 'It all went completely wrong that afternoon,' says Charlie, 'Gossip and I just missed it altogether.'

The whole performance started ominously when Charlie trotted a resisting, swan-necked Gossip in circles in the main arena, waiting for the bell to start his test. The steward, who let the competitors into and out of the arena at A, noticed Charlie wasn't wearing gloves, part of the compulsory dress. This fact he kindly pointed out to Charlie. Charlie, knowing that his and Gossip's efforts were hardly going to enthrall the judges, didn't feel the awful sinking feeling of panic that he should have done. He calmly trotted back to the collecting ring, where he found Lucinda and Mairangi, and borrowed her gloves.

I did not dare look as Charlie wheeled Gossip round to go back to the dressage arena. I felt sure Gossip would nap, having sighted one of his friends. For some extraordinary reason he didn't, but his head and neck were doing their best to impersonate a giraffe's.

The bell had rung, so Charlie had no alternative but to make the best of it. Resembling a Western horse on a cattle round-up, Gossip skittered through the movements of the test, guided by a resigned Charlie who knew he could do nothing to rectify the situation. Gossip's marks were more like a cricket score. He had run up a century – 101.4.

Charlie and Lucinda had given David a present of a sweater in thanks for his help with their dressage in the run-up to Badminton. When Charlie and David met after Gossip's test, David's only comment was, 'Well, I suppose I had better give you back the sleeves.'

As in Fontainebleau, Gossip was forgiven his appalling dressage when he had whisked Charlie over the massive Badminton fences to finish with a faultless and very fast round. Lucinda was pleased to see Charlie rewarding Gossip with big pats on his neck after each fence. In fact, Charlie was using the 'pats' as a way of galvanising impulsion. He felt that Gossip did not feel quite as fit as he had done in 1980 and needed some extra encouragement. A strong slap was a nicer way of asking than a tap with the whip, the latter being more beneficial in the approach to a fence or if a horse felt as though he might refuse.

Gossip had been placed bottom after the dressage, and with his treble-figure mark even his speed could not help him this time. He did, however, manage to move up to the mid-twenties.

On Sunday, working Gossip in for the show-jumping, Charlie was disconcerted at his horrible long, flat stride. This is a common occurrence in three-day event horses that are feeling stiff from the rigours of having jumped fixed fences at a fast, more onward-bound stride. Asking them for the bounce and precision required to clear show-jumps is like asking a marathon runner to run in a sprint race the day after he has covered thirty miles.

Charlie concentrated on softening and suppling Gossip, encouraging him to shorten and round his stride so that he jumped up over the show-jumps rather than across them. Charlie's efforts wrought a clear round out of Gossip but it still left them in only twenty-fourth place. It seemed that the dramatic days when he could overtake most of the field with his fantastic cross-country speed were coming to an end.

Lucinda had achieved clear rounds with both Killaire and Mairangi, and their vastly better dressage scores put them into tenth and sixth places respectively. But in the show-jumping Mairangi let everyone down by hitting three rails and dropping to twelfth. Lucinda felt disappointed that he lacked the enthusiasm he had begun to display in his spring one-day events.

Killaire had retained his place and during the prize-giving, at which Mark Phillips and Lincoln were the heroic victors, Killaire received a special round of warm-hearted applause when his retirement from international eventing was publicly announced.

The week after Badminton, Gossip and Mairangi went out for a holiday, and we said a sad goodbye to Killaire, who was leaving Appleshaw to take up permanent residence at his home in Sussex, where he was to enjoy some less demanding eventing with an up-and-coming young rider.

Charlie's other chief ride that spring was Ponch, who was being taken quietly round open intermediate tracks. At Tidworth he again caused some anxiety when he arrived home hopping lame, after finishing the cross-country sound. No obvious cause was found, until Paul thought he noticed some damage in the fetlock area on an X-ray. He injected Ponch's joint with synthetic joint-oil and a month later Ponch was sound.

Lucinda returned an ebullient Beagle Bay to the competition fray, but stopped short of doing a three-day event with him when a joint began crumbling suspiciously. Foxy, renamed Falmouth Bay having come into OCL ownership, took us over the Irish Sea to Punchestown, where he somewhat embarrassed Lucinda by running out at the ditch of the angled coffin, a problem Lucinda had warned the less-experienced riders competing at Punchestown to guard against. Foxy's gangly legs were caught out by another fence that involved two very acute turns, the second of which Foxy failed to make. Nor did he jump clear in the show-jumping, which makes his final placing of seventh rather unbelievable. It was his good fortune that almost everyone else was just as bad.

Lucinda decided to give him the 'Gossip' treatment and work him hard all year, thinking it might sharpen him up and discipline his concentration. So Foxy was packed off to the Luhmühlen three-day event, as Gossip had been in 1977. There he had his wits much more about him and finished ninth in a tough competition that included some of the best European and US riders and their horses.

During that summer, Charlie made the decision to move on to new pastures but the problem of finding a new co-jockey disappeared before it had even arrived. David Green returned from Australia, where he had been since his disappointment of 1980, and he brought back with him an Australian chestnut thoroughbred called Fair Deal. Although only six years old he had already raced and show-jumped to Grade B standard. David and Lucinda had bought him between them, and David had ridden him in his first three-day event that summer.

David slotted happily into life at Appleshaw, but even I was aware that David had not flown 12,000 miles just to take on Charlie's job.

Lucinda resumed riding Gossip when Charlie left, and he and Mairangi were put on the short-list for the European Championships in early September, at Horsens in Denmark.

Oddly, Gossip's eternal dressage problem did not plague Lucinda that summer. After his disastrous test at Badminton

Lucinda reckoned Gossip's dressage could not get much worse, so she relaxed, stopped fussing him and asked for absolutely nothing. Slowly but surely a revolutionary change took place. Gossip, finding he was not being dictated to, was puzzled, but gradually he unwound his coiled muscles as he realised there was no one to argue with. The tensions seeped out of him as his body loosened and relaxed. Very gingerly, he stretched out his neck to seek the bit and risk taking hold of it. At first he was wary of what it might do, but when it stayed softly still in his mouth his confidence grew.

At last, after six years of struggling, Lucinda and Gossip had broken through the mental barricades. This was what Herbert Rehbein had understood about Gossip in 1977, and was why he had made Gossip's flat-work look so mystifyingly easy. The key was to wait for Gossip to give, and not to ask first. And as Lucinda worked on Gossip, she discovered why Rehbein had said that if Gossip had been bigger, he would have had him for his dressage horse. Once Gossip was relaxed and comfortably on the bit, his naturally supple body produced some beautifully pleasing movements as he flowed through his paces.

This revelation in Gossip's dressage was as exciting as the discovery of how to ride him across country.

But when one thing comes right, something else usually goes wrong. At the first selection trial at Dauntsey, Gossip stopped twice in the treble in the show-jumping. Lucinda had over-steadied him, possibly temporarily forgetting it was Gossip, and Gossip felt he couldn't make the distance without his extra bit of speed. Lucinda reminded herself to give him his necessary power boost next time.

Mairangi and Beagle Bay covered themselves in rosettes at Dauntsey by winning their respective advanced sections, and Beagle Bay clinched his last-minute qualification for Burghley.

A fortnight later, Gossip, Mairangi and Foxy competed at Locko. As Lucinda trotted a calm sedate Gossip in fluent circles, other competitors watched in amazement. Rumours abounded that Lucinda had administered a new undetectable tranquilliser.

Lucinda still wasn't wholly certain that Gossip would keep up his relaxed profile in the arena, so she had cheated a little by putting him into a double bridle, on the purely tactical basis that it might encourage him to drop his chin. She continued to sit passively, asking no questions and applying no pressure.

Gossip was happy, and the atmosphere of the arena did not cause him to forsake his newly acquired security with the bit. He performed his best test ever, an incredible thirty marks better than his previous average scores.

Gossip's dressage was the only high spot of Locko for us. The rest of the proceedings fell about our ears in a series of painful disasters.

Maybe we should have heeded the warning of ill-fortune that happened on the drive up. Going to the rear of the horsebox to check the horses, I found that Gossip, bored with staring at mounds of luggage piled on the Luton shelf in front of him, had been rummaging. He had undone Lucinda's case and tugged out her lucky teddy, all of six inches high. Teddy was hanging out of Gossip's mouth, minus one button eye, which I guessed Gossip had swallowed. I disentangled a saliva-sodden bear from Gossip's jaws and told him not to tempt fate by chewing up his good-luck mascot. Gossip's answer was to flatten his ears at me and hammer on the partitions with his heels, furious at having his fun spoiled.

Gossip was Lucinda's first ride. He sped round the course in his usual style and was still clear as he approached the water complex, three fences from home. He jumped confidently up onto the sleeper platform, but suddenly his feet skidded as his hooves penetrated the three-inch layer of sand spread on top of the smooth wood. As he launched into the water six feet below on the landing side, he was still trying to readjust his balance lost in the skid. For a split second he seemed to have saved the situation, but his point of balance was too far forward and his knees buckled as his feet touched down. Head and neck disappeared, and Lucinda lurched off in a flurry of spray. Gossip's knees and his mouth scrunched against the sharp-edged stones on the river bed.

David and I had been waiting at the top of the hill, above

the water jump, by the finish. Hearing about Gossip's fall, over the loudspeaker, we jumped into the car and bumped quickly across the grass to the water jump. Gossip was being led out of the water by a kind elderly gentleman, a dazed and drenched Lucinda following. Gossip limped out, favouring his off-fore, blood streaming from his knees and a cut lip. Lucinda was upset and shocked that he had received so much injury. I took Gossip's reins and led him gently back to his stable. As I untacked him, Lucinda and David summoned a vet. An unhappy Gossip could only turn round in his stable by rearing back on his hind legs, as he tried to avoid putting weight on his off-fore. Peter Scott-Dunn examined Gossip and thought he might have chipped a bone, but only an X-ray would confirm or deny his prognosis. I bandaged up Gossip's knees, and positioned his haynet and water so that he did not have to turn round to reach them.

Gossip's fall was the first of many that day at the water jump, and Angela Tucker's Willow Pattern sustained almost identical injuries to Gossip's. The selectors began to panic, thinking they would have no horses left to choose from, and the fence was eliminated from the course for the remaining competitors. But this did not help Mairangi, who jumped all the other fences without apparent problem, but as his nanny, Ali Hicks, led him back into the stable yard, I saw he was holding up a hind leg. He was as lame behind as Gossip was in front.

Foxy actually managed to survive unscathed, and was the only one of Lucinda's rides to complete the competition. And so ended any thoughts and hopes of a trip to Denmark.

That evening, Gossip stared moodily into a corner of his stable, his backside firmly planted by the door to deter intruders. His knee hurt and his sore gums and lips made eating difficult. Sympathetic visitors were greeted by black glares and gnashing teeth, as his ears flattened back at the unwanted attention.

But the next day we had good news. The X-ray pictures showed no damage to Gossip's knee, and he was already, twenty-four hours later, more comfortable and able to walk round his stable without too much pain.

Mairangi's mystery lameness resolved itself into a severely twisted ankle, and after a few days the swelling and soreness began to decrease.

On future trips Gossip and teddy were kept well apart.

The deep bruising in and around Gossip's knee took close on two weeks to disperse. Amongst other treatments, Gossip was fed large amounts of arnica tablets, a homeopathic remedy to relieve bruising. The knee's progress was so promising, we thought Gossip would be fit enough to join Biggles in competing at Burghley.

The week before Burghley, Rushall's organiser, Barry Wookey, kindly let Lucinda school Gossip over his water jump, to allow Gossip to recover any loss of confidence he might have felt after Locko.

The day of our journey up to Burghley began in chaos. Lucinda overslept, I broke a Thermos that exploded glass all over me, we forgot the passports for the horses, and had to make a detour when we became snarled in a traffic jam. David and working pupil Camilla Cholmeley drove up at the eleventh hour with the necessary documents. Until the passports arrived, Gossip and Biggles had had to sit in temporary quarantine stables.

Lucinda and I then caused Gossip even more humiliation when he was 'spun' at the first vets' inspection that evening. We had stupidly only trotted him up at Appleshaw each day on a gravel surface, on which he had been sound. The hard, smooth tarmac of Burghley was unrelenting, and showed that there was possibly still some deep bruising from Locko that had not been drawn out.

Late that night, we had just wriggled into our sleeping bags, when someone called out to us, banging on the door of the horsebox: 'I think you had better come. Beagle Bay has stuck a leg through his stable wall.' We stumbled out to the darkened stables. Biggles dangled a hind leg pathetically. We hoped the damage was no more than bruising. Whilst I dug out a kaolin poultice and bandaged his leg, Lucinda and some helpful friends sought permission from the stable manager to move Biggles into one of the few permanent stables, before he smashed his present one to matchwood. After twenty minutes of huffing and puffing with bags of shavings, a new bed had been put down and I led Biggles to his new sleeping quarters. We flopped back into bed at a few minutes before midnight, and I crossed my fingers that surely nothing more had time to go wrong that day.

The next morning Gossip was driven home by a friend who lived near Appleshaw, in order to spare him the ordeal of having to watch the proceedings without being able to participate. A puzzled Gossip was bundled into a strange horsebox, unaccompanied by any familiar faces, and driven down to Hampshire. When David, who had returned to Appleshaw, after delivering the passports, went to collect Gossip from the friend's home, he found Gossip looking very dejected and miserable. David was convinced that Gossip thought he had been sold. His spirits did not revive until he was safely back in his own stable at Appleshaw, surrounded by people he knew.

Biggles had not badly injured his leg, and was completely sound the next morning. Over the next three days of the competition, he worked his way up until he was in the lead after the night of the cross country. But at a cost. He had hit the outside of his off-fore joint on a fence, and was feeling very sore from the subsequent bruising. My brother William, who had come up to help, traipsed back and forth to the caterers' tents, collecting bags of ice which we strapped round the swelling ankle. The treatment was effective, but not enough. That night, Lucinda phoned a faith-healer, as a last resort, and for five minutes we concentrated our positive thoughts onto Biggles' leg whilst the faith-healer did likewise.

Next morning Biggles was sound. Ice and faith, what a strange combination. He jumped clear in the afternoon and stood proudly in the main arena to receive the Raleigh Trophy, giving OCL their first major three-day event win.

Back home, Biggles joined Gossip in the field. Gossip was to have the rest of the year off to ensure his knee was given adequate time to settle, so there would be no niggling doubts when he came up again in January.

But life for the rest of us was still hectic. Foxy competed in his third three-day event of the year at Chesterland, Pennsylvania, home of Bruce Davidson. It was a fun, light-hearted trip, despite us grooms being quartered in a house that contained not a stick of furniture – we had to use a plank supported on a log and a window sill as a table, and some old drawers as seats. There were, at least, some beds and plenty of linen supplied by a local hospital.

The horses' stables were very precarious, temporary structures, under a brightly striped marquee. The individual stalls were so small that Foxy could only stand comfortably if he was on the diagonal. One day he attempted to roll, but he bent the slatted wooden sides to such an extent that it needed several strong men to straighten them.

Foxy very nearly bolted with me on the morning of his dressage when I was returning with him to the stables after a quiet hack. He saw a pack of the local hounds out on exercise, coming towards him. In his eyes they had to be pigs. Foxy fled up the road, as I hauled ineffectively on the reins.

Thankfully Foxy collected his wits together for his test, which was very polished and controlled. On cross-country day he suffered an attack of nerves before the start of phase A and it took three of us half an hour to resaddle him after Lucinda had weighed out. By the time he reached phase D he had sobered up, and with legs, body and brain all working in unison for once, he finished with a fast clear round. He completed the competition with a clear in the show-jumping to finish third, and our estimation of his prowess shot up several notches.

It was only when he flew back to England that a suspiciously warm leg confirmed itself as a strained tendon. Unlike Gossip, he hadn't quite been able to stand up to such a rigorous programme. He would have to be given the next six months off.

Mairangi, Ponch and David's Fair Deal went to Boekelo. So did a mountainous stack of telegrams and cards. Only days before, Lucinda and David had announced their engagement.

At Boekelo Ponch began to prove he wasn't such a wasted investment, by racing round the course at 'Gossip' speed but with an even scopier jump, and took second place. His dressage, although not good, was far less of a nightmare than

Gossip's because Ponch never saw dressage as anything to become worked up about. His chief problem lay in the fact that he sucked back, behind the bit, his sides dead to Lucinda's leg aids. Dressage bored Ponch, and as he had none of the natural movement Gossip could now produce, he considered the whole business a waste of time. It was only his generous, honest nature that tolerated Lucinda's persistence when schooling him.

Mairangi, Lucinda had discovered, had a lung problem; they had been overstretched at Lexington, which had made them less elastic. With the aid of an inhalant, Cromovet, and a bulk-free diet to reduce pressure on the lungs, Mairangi was a new horse. In place of hay, he was fed quantities of carrots, which Ali and I offered him in relays on the journey to and from Boekelo, while the others munched at their haynets. Mairangi was seventh at Boekelo, and he enjoyed every minute he was competing.

David had to coax a rather green Fair Deal round the course, collecting two refusals en route, but the experience gained far outweighed the addition of faults.

Two days after arriving back from Boekelo, Ponch became very ill. He refused to eat, his temperature soared and he was not passing dung or urine. He had contracted a travel virus, as Discovery Bay had done in 1979, but Ponch's had been accentuated by his body feeling tired from the exertions of the event.

A two-gallon saline solution, tubed into his stomach, had an instantaneous effect. Everything started to work and the next day I took three barrow-loads of soaking shavings from his bed. A week later, he was able to join the others in the field.

1981 ended on a note of great happiness with Lucinda's and David's wedding in early December, after which they flew out for a honeymoon and holiday in the warm sunshine of Kenya.

10   Return to the Homeland

At fourteen years old, Gossip bounced back to the eventing scene, *his* sights firmly set on Badminton. But two other horses were also being prepared for Badminton 1982 – Ponch and Biggles. When the forms arrived in February, Lucinda entered all three. Lucinda particularly wanted to ride Ponch at Badminton; he was her most promising prospect for future team selection but he needed to prove himself round a big course to stand any chance of being considered. Of the other two, Lucinda was unsure which she was happy to leave behind. Gossip, now in the evening of his career, could perhaps have only one more crack at the championship before the wear and tear of years and age caught up with him. But Beagle Bay was only two years younger, and had not yet tackled Badminton. Both horses stood an equal chance of success.

It was an enviable situation to have such a choice and at this early stage in the year, but Lucinda doubted she would be forced into a decision. However careful and well-planned the preparation for a three-day event, luck plays an important part and there is always the risk of lameness from even a minor injury such as a bruised foot.

David was entered for Badminton on Mairangi, whom he was to take over now that Lucinda was so involved with the other three. He also had the ride on a gentle giant of 17 hh called Chili Con Carne, who was owned by Major Lycett.

Gossip's first outing of the spring was to the last holding of the Downlands Horse Trials at Liphook in Hampshire, for the open intermediate class. He scorched round the undemanding cross country, disdainfully clipping the tops of most of the fences with his hooves, his way of saying the course was too easy. Lucinda had mistakenly thought he should have a gentle first event, after the shock of his last round at Locko. But Gossip was so frustrated at not being able to stretch himself, he was in a dreadful mood when he arrived back at the horsebox for his wash-down. Ali, who was helping David with his horses, came to the rescue to hold him. She was dragged and shoved from side to side, as Gossip wriggled away from my ministrations with sponge and water, and tried to kick the bucket over with some carefully aimed swipes. By the time I had finished, Gossip had towed Ali some fifty yards from the horsebox, and had cleared the area of all spectators and competitors within a twenty-yard radius.

I was thankful that Gossip's next event would be the tough advanced course of Rushall, which would really give him something to think about.

On the intervening weekend between Downlands and Rushall, Ponch, Biggles, Mairangi and Chili went to Frensham.

Mr. and Mrs. Green turned the cross-country phase into a race against the clock. First went Ponch, who did not waste a second, and finished with a fast clear. David and Mairangi then proceeded to make a mockery of Ponch's time, and finished clear, ten seconds faster. Chili clocked up the same time as Ponch, so Lucinda really had to sit down and ride Biggles and she just succeeded in holding off David's attack. Ponch and Biggles won their respective advanced sections, and Mairangi and Chili would have been close runners-up if they had not both hit a rail in the show-jumping.

At Rushall, Lucinda was down to ride Gossip, Biggles and her new acquisition, the diminutive but very strong Masterpiece, jointly owned by OCL and David Mason. Husband David had Mairangi and another of Lucinda's ex-rides, Botany Bay. Their cross-country times were fairly close together as all the horses were running in the advanced class, and Ali and I were running around like demented dervishes. Our problem wasn't helped by the fact that we had not been able to park our two horseboxes next to each other. As Ali and I ran from one horsebox to another with tack, boots and bandages, Rosemary Hicks, Ali's mother, offered her services as seamstress. We organised ourselves: I wound bandages round ten fore legs, Rosemary followed me, deftly sewing the ends, while Ali strapped cross-country boots onto ten hind legs. As soon as one horse was ready, Lucinda or David were legged aboard and it seemed no time before they were back again with a puffing sweaty mount and needing the next one. Gossip, naturally, caused a disruption by napping and I had to stop the bandaging and run across the field to start him. I'm sure he did it deliberately, knowing how rushed we were.

But by tea-time the last horse had been washed down, dried and rugged-up, and was contentedly chewing at his haynet. As Ali and I cleared up the sea of saddlery, boots and grubby bandages surrounding the horseboxes, Lucinda and David walked back from the prize-giving clutching a fistful of rosettes and Midland Bank cheques. I forgave Gossip his misbehaviour. After a lovely test, he had overtaken Biggles with a faster time on the cross country and pushed his stablemate into second place. Mairangi had been second for David in the other section and Botany Bay was seventh.

The day after Rushall all five Badminton contenders were fit and well. Although Lucinda was happy that her three were in good shape there was no pointer as to which she should leave behind. This meant that Gossip and Biggles would have to continue their fitness work right up to three-day peak, although one of them would not have to make use of it.

It was still so easy for something to go wrong, be it a simple mishap in the field or stable as happened to Killaire in 1980.

The next two weeks slipped by without incident. On the Monday morning of Badminton week, I began packing the trunks for four horses. That evening, I asked Lucinda if she had decided. Staring out of the window of her office, Lucinda muttered, 'We'll take Ponch and Biggles tomorrow, but Gossip will be brought up for the vets' inspection. Let's wait until they have all passed that safely.' Although it was not possible to ride three horses at a three-day event, it was permissible to trot up three horses, after which one would have to be withdrawn.

On Tuesday, Ali, who was looking after Mairangi, and myself climbed into the horsebox. Gossip stared after us, ears pricked in enquiry, a worried and disappointed expression on his face. Why wasn't he going too?

On Wednesday afternoon, I was plaiting Ponch at Badminton for the vets' inspection, when I heard a horsebox being parked outside. From the thumps and bangs coming from its interior I could guess who was inside. Camilla, who was to look after Chili for the duration of the event, had brought Gossip. As she unloaded him, I saw Gossip's bright expectant face. His relief was obvious, 'Oh, I haven't been forgotten after all.'

Between us we manoeuvred all five up to the inspection area in front of Badminton House. As Lucinda led Gossip up to the ground jury, he seemed to grow in stature, peering about him with a knowing air. This was where he rightfully should be. As Lucinda led him to the end of the gravel sweep and turned to trot him past the ground jury, Gossip could not resist a squeal of excitement and happiness as he bounded past.

Ponch, Biggles and Gossip had all passed, as had David's two. Lucinda was left in an agony of indecision. Biggles won.

It was left to two Australians to take a horrified, mystified and very, very angry Gossip back to Appleshaw, Jill Rymill, our resident grook (cook cum groom), and Helen Carr, a working pupil, had come up with Camilla and Gossip in order that after watching the inspection, they could take the spare horse back home.

The entire journey back, Gossip kicked and thrashed, all but spitting with rage. When they unloaded him at Appleshaw, he was in such a temper that they could not change his travel clothes, and they had to leave him in his stable for an hour to calm down. Gossip's anger melted into a deeply wounded hurt. What had he done wrong to be so swiftly removed from the party he had just been taken up to join? Life was incomprehensible. He did, however, gain some small consolation; he had two hapless Aussies at his mercy, and whenever they tried to enter his stable he had great satisfaction in letting loose some powerful double-barrelled hooves, which sent Jill and Helen straight out again in a state of near-hysterical fear mingled with sympathetic laughter as they tried to pacify him.

Gossip gradually regained his composure and humour and was comforted by Sue Jackson, who had looked after him during the spring of 1981 and at that year's Badminton. Sue had left but had kindly agreed to return and help Jill and Helen with the horses, whilst we were at Badminton.

Chili performed the best dressage test of the four, coming tenth overall; the other three were not too far behind him. A hectic cross-country day resulted in the thrill of four clear rounds, but success was clouded by Chili's severe lameness that evening. Although never putting a foot wrong, his heavy, hunter-type body, combined with his straight-arm landing technique, must have exerted too much pressure on a suspensory ligament over one of the drop fences. His leg was heavily bandaged and he was withdrawn.

On Sunday, Mairangi cheered David up by jumping clear and taking sixth place, Ponch was seventh and Biggles eighth. If Chili had been able to jump, he could well have finished ninth.

Gossip could hardly keep the gloating expression off his face the week after Badminton, when he was brought back into work after a week lazing in the field, whilst the others were roughed off.

He and Masterpiece, and Botany Bay for David, were all entered for the Punchestown three-day event in the third week of May.

All three competed at Bicton Horse Trials in Devon. The day was typically spring-like, bursts of bright sunshine, interspersed with sudden downpours. Gossip was feeling lighthearted and flippant, and fooled around in his dressage, changing legs in his counter canter. Botany Bay was no better behaved for David in the show-jumping, and knocked down four fences, leaving David very despondent about Punchestown, where Botany Bay would have to show-jump and be feeling tired and stiff from the cross country the previous day.

The cross-country going became very slick, as rain fell on the firm ground. When Helen, on her own Champagne Charlie, slipped and fell at a downhill fence, Lucinda asked

Ali and I to screw studs into the horses' front shoes to help them grip. Gossip and Botany Bay redeemed themselves with clear rounds across country, but it was little Masterpiece who came out on top and won the advanced class, with Gossip third.

The week before Punchestown, the three went to Stowell Park event just for the dressage and show-jumping phases. Matters went from bad to worse. Gossip was eliminated in the show-jumping as Lucinda started before the bell, and David had to retire in the dressage.

Botany Bay, who had been working well outside the arena, decided in the middle of his test, that half-passes were an impossibility. He was a very neurotic horse so I wasn't surprised to see him start to rear. But then he flatly refused to continue to do anything but stand on his hind legs, which was a little disconcerting. David tactfully retired, and was allowed to work him in the arena after the dressage had finished. Botany Bay behaved angelically as though he had done nothing wrong. David took a philosophical view of the incident, but could see there was no reason why it should not reoccur in the tense atmosphere of the arena at Punchestown.

In the final week before Punchestown, Gossip ran up light, looking more like a racehorse. He was never easy to keep weight on, and he always lost unnecessary pounds with his excessive energies on the gallops. The fitter he became, the more finicky he was in his eating habits. He liked his diet to be very well balanced, with equal proportions of oats and nuts, and not too large a feed. If I tried to give him an extra quantity of either, he would immediately stop eating altogether, and it might take two or three days before he would clear up his full rations.

His leanness had not been helped by the fact that he had been three-day-event fit in April, and it had been quite a juggling act to prevent him going over the top and becoming stale through May.

The horsebox was bulging with the three horses, tack trunks, feed, hay, luggage and four people squashed into the cab. After a calm, uneventful crossing from Fishguard to Rosslare in southern Ireland, we drove up past the Wicklow mountains, scene of Gossip's birth, and into the precincts of Punchestown racecourse where the event was staged. We had arrived on the Wednesday evening and the vets' inspection was to be on the Friday. There was to be only one day of dressage at Punchestown, due to the small entry of thirty-odd runners. Cross-country day was on Sunday, principally because Saturday racing in Ireland holds as popular a rating as does football in England, and the organisers hoped to attract a larger crowd than they might have done otherwise.

Gossip found he had several fans in this, his first visit to his homeland since 1975, as many Irish eventing enthusiasts had followed his career closely from that time. And his staunchest fan was Katie, who had come to watch him. She was thrilled to see Goose looking contented in his new life with us, but Gossip had not forgotten his friend and saviour, and he nuzzled Katie affectionately as though she had left only yesterday.

Gossip and Masterpiece were quite happy in the racecourse stables, but Botany Bay panicked as he could not see his friends from his box. He rushed round his stable yelling, and weaved madly over the door. David contrived to move him to a box opposite the other two and he did settle a little. It was good that Ali with her calm patient attitude was looking after him, and she did well to keep his dottiness at bay.

Lucinda was riding Masterpiece first, and his dressage was one of the earliest of the day. The little horse was becoming very tense and strong in his dressage if he felt pressurised by his rider, so he was only hacked before his test, with Lucinda collecting him up just a few minutes before he went in. The method worked and an agreeable mark put him third.

Ali and I held our breath and crossed our fingers when David entered the arena on Botany Bay. With the skilful tact of a diplomat, David eased him through the movements, and nudged him with the softest of aids into the half-passes. Botany Bay responded in similar vein, and looked very peaceable and happy. Ali had spent some time lungeing him earlier, which had contributed to his relaxed state of mind. Botany Bay earned a good enough mark to take him into sixth place at the end of the day.

In the afternoon there were some good tests from the more

seasoned stars of the event world. Heading the cast was Bruce Davidson on his Lexington star, Might Tango. Bruce had originally intended to ride the big grey at Badminton but had had to withdraw, and so, like Gossip, had come to Ireland. In a light-hearted moment after Badminton, Lucinda had bet Bruce that Gossip would beat Tango at Punchestown. If I hadn't known it was a joke, I would have had serious doubts about Lucinda's sanity as Bruce was nearly always in the first three after the dressage, and Tango's reliable performances would be sure to put him there again.

True to form, Bruce and Tango produced a foot-perfect test that put them into the lead.

Then came Gossip. Since the dramatic breakthrough last summer, his dressage had become more and more consistent. That afternoon in Punchestown, he was in an exceptionally sunny mood, enjoying the informal atmosphere. He swept through his test with the charisma of a showman and the elegant grace of a thoroughbred. When his score went up on the board, he had beaten Might Tango by a single point.

We spent the next few hours in a trance of disbelief. For Gossip to lead after the dressage in a three-day event was something we thought could only happen in a dream. Katie was convinced that Gossip could not help but win the event, now that he had conquered the hitherto impossible.

How could he fail, when his cross country and show-jumping had always pulled him up in the placings?

Cross-country day was furiously busy. Because of the small entry there was only a period of about ten minutes between Masterpiece finishing phase D, and Gossip starting on phase A. But one of the reasons why I liked Punchestown so much was the convenience of the starts for each phase. The phase A start was just behind the stables; a short walk to the left of the grandstand brought you to the start of phase B. (Since 1984, it has been moved and can only be reached in time by car.) The checkpoint at the end of the steeplechase was in the same area, and the Box before phase D was only a few minutes' walk on from there.

Early in the morning, Ali and I lugged the bulk of the necessary equipment up to the Box, and kept two bucketfuls of spares at the stables, one for each of us, for use on the first three phases. Ali was then committed to Botany Bay for the rest of the day and was unable to help me, as he was competing between Lucinda's two rides.

I saw Lucinda off on phase A on Masterpiece then scuttled back to the stables to tidy up and lay out his rugs and stable bandages for when he finished. Then, collecting a spares bucket, I headed for the steeplechase start and checked that all was in order when Lucinda came off A. They had no problems on phase B, and, as they trotted past me on phase C, I gave a thumbs-up sign to Lucinda that all was OK. I had half an hour before I needed to be in the Box, so I quickly returned to the stables, put on Gossip's bridle and back boots and screwed studs into his shoes. His cross-country bandages on his front legs were already in place, and he needed only the saddle that was on Masterpiece, with a change of numnah. Leaving Gossip tied up looking rather disgruntled at this 'Pony Club' treatment, I grabbed the spares bucket again and sped up to the Box.

As Lucinda and Masterpiece trotted in off phase C, Masterpiece appeared stiff in his quarters as he came towards us. Lucinda wasn't happy either. We hastily threw a rug over his loins, and gave him only a cursory wash-down with warm water, so he could walk round the Box and stop his muscles from stiffening up further. He had to stand, though, whilst I quickly smeared grease down his legs, before legging Lucinda aboard. The momentary pause made him appear cramped again, but after Lucinda had trotted a couple of circles in the Box, he looked and felt normal, and Lucinda presented him at the start. He cleared the first four fences, but fence five, a series of steps up with a rail at the top, proved beyond him. His hindquarters were definitely not working properly, and Lucinda retired.

When she reached the Box, I flung a thick rug over him, and led him back to the stables while Lucinda consulted a vet. Untacking Masterpiece, I glanced at my watch. Eight minutes before Gossip was due to start on phase A. I snatched Masterpiece's saddle, yanked undone the soggy numnah and shot into Gossip's stable. Dry numnah and saddle in place, I silently summoned my limited powers of patience and dexterity as I fumbled with breast-plate and girth buckles beside a fidgeting, excited Gossip, who was humping his back and firing a rapid salvo of cow-kicks, which I somehow avoided. I was tugging at the girth straps as Lucinda sprinted across the yard, Gossip's number-cloth half way over her head. An anxious vet hurried in her wake, but I had to leave him with Masterpiece as there were less than five minutes to have Gossip at the start and no guarantee that he would agree to go if I was not attached to him with a lead rein. I legged Lucinda up and she let the reins sit on his neck as she stuffed fingers into dry gloves. I encouraged Gossip into a brisk jog to the start. Fortunately Gossip had become fed up with being ignored and was so eager for action that he forgot about his nerves and napping. We jogged straight into the start box and immediately out again, minus me, as Lucinda picked up the reins for the first time and steered Gossip onto phase A.

Gossip safely despatched, I ran back to the stables to see what the vet had to say about Masterpiece. Thankfully, he did not feel it was the onset of azoturia as Masterpiece had walked back to the stables without any sign of increased stiffening. There was no need for any treatment. So I changed Masterpiece's rugs for dry ones, and took off his cross-country boots and bandages. As I began to remove the worst of the grease from his legs with a towel, I saw from my watch that I should be on my way to the start of phase B for Gossip. A surprised Masterpiece stared after my second flurried exit from his stable. Spares bucket in one hand and start rein in the other, I wriggled through the roving spectators and plonked down the bucket as Gossip came through the flags at the finish of phase A. He knew exactly what came next and his nerves were gaining the upper hand. He saw me approaching with the start rein and backed off with half rears so I could not reach his head. 'Thirty seconds,' called the steward. I lunged at Gossip's reins in a moment when his front feet were on the ground, and had the rein through his bit rings before he realised it. He then wouldn't turn round, so I reversed him across to the phase B start. Lucinda could do nothing; any interference from her would have made his napping far worse.

As the countdown came to 'three. . .' we edged into the start box, and I began to slip the rein from the bit rings. Gossip reared up towards me, but I could not dodge out from the box as its sides were solid brushwood. I ducked to avoid his feet, and we missed colliding. 'Go!' boomed the steward, and Lucinda let Gossip onto the course.

Due to a measurement discrepancy on the steeplechase, a complaint had been lodged by a competitor and the hasty alteration, only threequarters of an hour before the cross country began, resulted in the time on phase B being so easy to make that riders were walking by the time they passed through the finish. Gossip, being his usual jet-propelled self, was pulled to a walk way before the finish flags, and was barely blowing by the time he met me to check him at the start of phase C.

That done, I beetled back to the stables, where Masterpiece showed no surprise at my sudden reappearance. I seized the towel again, finished cleaning his legs, and wrapped them in bandages. He displayed no signs of discomfort and I felt happy to leave him chewing on a haynet while I attended to Gossip in the Box. As I made my way to the Box area, I heard over the loudspeakers that David was on the course and sounded to be having an excellent ride. Ali was waiting at the end of phase D and she reported that Botany Bay had experienced no problems so far. We watched David jump the last fence and delightedly pat Botany Bay as they galloped through the finish. A clear round and, amazingly, inside the time – Botany Bay was not considered a fast horse. Lucinda, out on phase C, had heard the commentary and was equally surprised at his fast time. She concluded that the time could not be too hard to make, and as Gossip was always in a hurry, she did not feel she would have to watch the clock too closely.

Washing down Gossip in the Box, we heard Bruce having an unhappy time with Might Tango, as the commentator reported a second refusal. Yet another victim of Lexington. The horse had never shown the same outstanding form since then. Lucinda's joke bet was forgotten; the fun had gone out of the challenge.

Gossip was more amenable at the start of phase D, and I let

him go onto the cross country without risk of being knocked out by waving hooves.

'Hmmm,' muttered David, who was waiting with me at the end of the course, timing Gossip with his stopwatch. 'Could be in for a few time faults.'

Gossip was. He went clear and kept his lead, but he had added six time faults to his score. He was now less than a show-jump ahead of the horse lying second – Botany Bay, the only horse to have no time faults, with Gossip the next fastest.

Gossip was lame that evening with a sore and reddened heel, where he must have galloped over a stony patch. Three other British horses had similar problems, but Botany Bay was fine. I ransacked the beer tent for ice-cubes, and Ali kept up a supply of kettles of hot water. We sat up much of the night tubbing Gossip's foot to disperse the bruising. The following morning, trotting on a tarmac road, he was sound.

That afternoon, a small but enthusiastic crowd lined the arena for the final phase. The show-jumping course was proving troublesome, and when Botany Bay went in to jump, there had been only one clear round, from Mark Hall on Herringfleet. Ironically, Mark had missed walking the course and only learnt of its problems from watching the other riders.

As David prepared to start his round there was only Gossip left to jump. A steward came up to me and asked if I was Gossip's groom. I nodded. 'Well now, if you'll give me your name,' he began, 'there's a prize for the groom of the winning horse.'

'Oh, that's a little premature, don't you think?' I smiled back. 'After all, the competition is not over yet.'

One thing I had learnt over the years was never to assume anything, and that no competition is won until the last fence has been jumped.

I pointed to Ali, standing nearby. 'It's always possible you might need this person's name instead.'

David made full use of his natural show-jumping talents and conjured an unbelievable clear round out of Botany Bay, who had flattened half of the Bicton course only three weeks before.

Gossip threw in his last surprise of the competition and

thumped the gate at fence three to the ground, and registered his fourth second place in a three-day event.

David, Botany Bay and Ali more than deserved their victory. They had all put in their best every inch of the way.

Riding Gossip back to the stables after the prize-giving, he jiggled and jogged, unbothered as I admonished him for being such a clot and missing his chance, which I felt sure he would never come so close to again.

He tucked into his tea, oblivious to the fuss and excitement in the yard, as a beaming Ali rode in on Botany Bay who looked a little bashful at all the sudden attention.

Little Masterpiece peered over his door, where he had spent a boring afternoon in the deserted stable yard. I put a headcollar on him and led him out to graze, all traces of stiffness now disappeared, and happy that I was now free to give him some attention.

Back in England the trio revelled in a late spring holiday, and Ponch came back into work in preparation for the World Championships in Luhmühlen in the autumn.

11 Gossip Goes West Again

The first selection trial at Dauntsey was thwarted by rock-like ground from a heatwave in the last part of July. None of the short-listed riders wanted to risk their horses, so the selectors had to rely on past form, and the imminent trials at Locko, to choose their team.

To Locko, Lucinda took Ponch, Biggles and Masterpiece. David, by special request, was allowed to ride Mairangi there. Locko, being the National Championships, was open only to British riders. David, with Mairangi, had been selected for the Australian team and badly needed a warm-up competition.

We had mixed fortunes at Locko, though none of the horrid ordeals of the previous year. David had a heavy fall with Mairangi in the show-jumping, when the horse's legs became entangled in the last part of a combination and they crashed to the ground. Fortunately they both survived unscathed.

Masterpiece put in an unexpected stop at the revamped water jump, possibly taken by surprise, as it involved jumping from light into dark shadows.

Biggles, after a brilliant dressage, set off on the cross country in pursuit of the title. Lucinda took a risk at the water, the penultimate fence, and paid the penalty at the last, a simple birch fence, when Biggles missed his stride, hiccupped through the fence and deposited Lucinda on the ground the other side. He cantered up the course towards the finish, and I ran out and grabbed his rein as he tried to dodge past. I was almost jerked off my feet as I forced him to a halt, then I ran back down the hill with him to Lucinda. No damage was done and as I legged Lucinda back up so she could ride through to finish, we both laughed with relief –

something always goes wrong at Locko, but at least this time there had been no serious injury.

Ponch avoided all the pitfalls and finished runner up to the winners, Ginny Holgate on Priceless. The next morning, he trotted up sound and was allotted his place on the team.

There was consternation in the yard when we returned to Appleshaw. Helen Carr's little horse had contracted a virus and was put into immediate isolation, in our next-door neighbour's only stable. The horses returning from Locko were stabled in the top yard, all of fifty yards from the bottom one, in the faint hope that the germ would not spread. Gossip, who had been stabled near Helen's horse, had to stay where he was, and we hoped his tough constitution would throw off any invading infection.

We were very lucky. Nobody evidenced so much as a sniffle.

The week before we left for Luhmühlen, Lucinda and David rode five horses between them at Rotherfield Horse Trials. Here, Gossip pulled his best and most original trick ever. He entered the dressage arena, trotted up the centre line, halted at X, and staled. Lucinda wasn't aware of what he was doing at first, and couldn't think why he refused to move but just shuffled his legs. Then she heard the sound of gushing liquid. The dressage judges could hardly see for tears of laughter, and Lucinda began to giggle. When Gossip was feeling more comfortable, he calmly proceeded with his test, indifferent to the suppressed chuckles of mirth from his rider.

Back at the horsebox, I changed his tack ready for the show-jumping. Lucinda mounted, and I climbed inside the lorry to tack up her next ride, Masterpiece. Outside Gossip was behaving appallingly, and he refused to budge an inch towards the show-jumping ring.

'Do you want any help?' I called from the Luton head, where I was trying to put a bridle on.

'Yes, please,' came a wail. I jumped down.

'No, don't worry, I think we are going . . . ' I climbed back onto the Luton.

'Help, we're stuck again . . . Oh no, it's OK. We're off . . . Oh, Gossip!'

This carried on for five minutes, and I leapt in and out of the lorry like a yo-yo. At length I ran behind him, chivvying away like a hen. Once Lucinda had him in a spanking trot, she kept it up until she reached the show-jumping arena.

I made sure I had time to start him on the cross country, and he finished fifth with the fastest time of the day.

This book is about Gossip. But the 1982 World Championships cannot be dismissed in a mere sentence or two. The competition developed into one of the tightest finishes, with fortunes bouncing between the British, the Americans and the Germans, like a ping-pong ball. Despite the intense rivalry, there remained a cheerful, friendly atmosphere between officials, riders and grooms, and this camaraderie lasted throughout the week of the Championships. Only one black cloud overshadowed the week, that of the tragic death of the Swiss rider Ernst Baumann, who had been fatally pinned under his horse when they fell at the last water jump. Before the show-jumping phase, a tribute was paid to him and the Swiss flag lowered to half mast.

The British horses had performed magnificently across country and held the team lead from the Americans and the Germans, but only by a nail-biting 2.2 points. Ponch had exceeded all our wildest expectations, and had streaked into second place behind Helmut Rethemeier of Germany on Santiago.

David and Mairangi had performed their best dressage ever, to stand sixth overall, but a harmless fall on the cross country added heavy penalties to their score.

The tension was almost unbearable as the show-jumping commenced. Busy with the horses in the background, we could not see what was happening, but the gasps, cheers and groans from the packed stands gave us virtually a running commentary.

Ponch kangarooed his way over the huge course, but I thought all was lost as he came into the last parallel fighting the bit and on a wrong stride. I should have had more faith.

Lucinda kicked and Ponch stood off. He sailed over and galloped through to the finish to cheering, rapturous applause at his clear round.

When Helmut went in, the atmosphere made muscles turn to jelly, the air of expectancy hung so heavily. The home crowd could hardly contain their anguish as Santiago rattled rails which settled back into their cups. Then the first rail fell at the combination. He could not afford another one down if he was to stay in the lead. Helmut steadied and balanced his horse for the second part of the combination. A rail clattered to the ground.

I hugged my little four-legged champion of the world.

And the British team stayed ahead. Team Captain Richard Meade on Kilcashel, going last, ensured they did, dropping only one rail which still kept the Brits ahead of the Germans, who had overtaken the Americans as they had in Lexington.

Back to earth with a bump. We had no time to rest on our laurels. Ali and I returned from Luhmühlen on Tuesday evening with Ponch and Mairangi. On Wednesday morning, we had to be ready to leave for Burghley with Biggles, Botany Bay and Gossip. There was a mountain of washing, trunks needed sorting and repacking, and the horsebox had to be loaded with hay and feed.

Gossip was not going to run at Burghley. He had received an invitation to compete at Chesterland in two weeks' time and was coming to Burghley so that Lucinda could catch up on his work, which had been neglected the week of Luhmühlen.

I felt guilty at deserting Ponch so soon, but he seemed happy enough in the field with Mairangi at the start of their long winter break.

Biggles and Gossip both had permanent stables at Burghley, in deference to their atrocious kicking habits.

Biggles, as defending champion, was under a certain amount of pressure to win again, but with the euphoria of Luhmühlen still about us, it seemed positively indecent to be lucky enough to collect another first so soon. When Biggles fumbled his stride and had to stop at a bounce complex, he effectively doused any such hopes and ultimately finished the competition in ninth place overall.

David's luck had been left in Ireland. The Trout Hatchery, notorious for giving riders a ducking, added David and Botany Bay to its list of victims. They finished the course, but Botany Bay was found to have a strained tendon that night. (It was the end of Botany Bay's eventing career, but he is now enjoying life as a joint-master's horse.)

Gossip's final gallop before Chesterland was to be on grass gallops, by kind permission of Toby Balding. These were sited just outside Weyhill village, a short hack from Appleshaw by road. Lucinda's daily schedule meant she was always running a race against the clock, so I hacked him up there and she was to meet me in the car.

Gossip was bursting with energy and, from the direction in which we were heading, he had a fair idea of what he was going to do. He thought about napping as I crossed the first road, and I hustled him across at a trot before he had time to think harder. But at the next junction, the track on the other side of the road led directly to the gallops. Gossip's nerves took over. He spun away and started to bounce up and down on his hind legs. Every time I tried to turn him round, he reared then stamped his foot. It was the best argument he had enjoyed for ages. It was too risky to back him across the road, and he was becoming wise to that trick. So we continued to bob up and down on the roadside, and as our tempers flared, Gossip reversed into a road sign and almost sat in a drainage ditch. I was so cross I gave him a hefty wallop on his backside, which made him shoot forward, only to dig his toes in even more adamantly at the edge of the road. It was no good. I had to give up and wait for Lucinda.

Gossip stood on the grass verge, all but humming a tune, as he gazed about nonchalantly resting a hind foot. A car came to a halt behind us. Lucinda merely raised her eyebrows, guessing accurately what Gossip had been up to. I dismounted and gave her a leg up. Gossip now had no choice but to go forward, as I could 'whip-in' behind him. He scuttled across the road, and I chased him all the way down the track, in case he had second thoughts.

* * * *

At nine o'clock on a Sunday evening Gossip and I, with Clarissa Strachan's Delphy Kingfisher, and his groom Sandra, who were also going to Chesterland, left on the first leg of our journey to the USA.

The event was beginning on Thursday with the vets' inspection in the afternoon. There would be only one day of dressage. To be leaving the UK when we were, was cutting things a little fine, as both horses had to undergo a period of quarantine and would not be released until the results of routine blood tests were known. This meant that the earliest our horses would be returned to us was Wednesday morning, assuming there were no delays.

The horsebox that collected us from Appleshaw arrived at Stansted airport at midnight. Take-off time was scheduled for three o'clock in the morning. The entire plane was to be filled with horses, leaving a few seats at the rear for some professional flying grooms, and the likes of Sandra and myself. The other horses on the trip were all youngstock, bound for the racetrack. We were also to land in Ireland en route, to pick up mares and foals at Shannon airport.

As we drew up in the parking bay at Stansted, two waiting horseboxes showed up in the glare of our headlights. Presumably, they contained the youngstock. An agent from the company handling the travel arrangements came over and took what papers we had regarding Gossip and Kingfisher. After this initial flurry of activity, there was little sign of life and, peering through the drizzle on the windscreen, I couldn't even see an aircraft. I had my doubts about our schedule running to time.

Gossip and Kingfisher were unconcerned at being stuck in a horsebox in the middle of the night, both being seasoned travellers, and they munched steadily on their hay. Their hard-feed rations had been cut drastically over the last thirty-six hours to minimise the risk of colic or azoturia.

Sandra and I snatched some sleep in the living area of the horsebox and were woken around 5.30 am by the sound of voices ordering the horsebox drivers to bring their lorries out onto the tarmac of the loading area. Rubbing the sleep from our eyes, we glimpsed a solitary plane through the dank mist.

To load the horses, they had first to be led up a long, quite steep ramp into the plane. They then had to be walked down the length of the fuselage, turned, then backed into a compartment consisting of movable wooden boards that were slotted into place around them once the horse was in position.

Gossip was grumpy as I led him out into the drizzle, a sure sign he was tired, and he still had an eight-hour flight in front of him. One of his cow-kicks had already caught me on the knee as I fumbled with his rugs.

He scrambled obligingly after me up the ramp, but snapped his teeth at the other grooms as they swiftly placed the partitions round him. One of them tried to pat him and Gossip flattened his ears and bucked bad-temperedly. I decided to hobble him as the partitions did not look over strong and I didn't want him being a nuisance on the flight.

Meanwhile the professional flying grooms were loading the youngstock. What a nightmare it must have seemed for the yearlings, who had seen so little of the outside world. I was very impressed at the quiet efficient manner of loading them and, surprisingly, very few of them played up.

Sandra and I gathered up extra haynets, rugs and spare headcollars for the journey. The limited seating area in the plane was fairly cramped, and our tempers began to fray as we stumbled back and forth along the narrow aisle that ran the length of the plane beside the horses.

At last all horses and humans were loaded and the hatches shut. Gossip was damp with sweat from the near-stifling temperatures, so I had to remove all his rugs. Then, as the engines rumbled to life, the air-conditioning came on and within seconds the temperature dropped by ten degrees, and I hastily draped a rug over his back. Every time I did something to him, he humped his back and bucked, furious at being pestered yet again, but I was worried he would catch a chill.

It was 9 am by the time we taxied to the end of the runway; twelve hours since we had left Appleshaw. By now we should have been halfway across the Atlantic, and we still had to stop in Ireland. I began to wonder if we would have Gossip and Kingfisher through quarantine and down to Chesterland in time for their dressage.

An hour later, Sandra and I were eating breakfast in Shannon's airport lounge whilst the mares and foals were loaded. The temperature inside the aircraft shot up and then down again, and Gossip railed in a black fury as I put rugs on or took them off.

The mares were sensible to load and the foals stuck close to their mothers, who were given wide compartments. During the flight there was a moment of worry when one of the foals slipped and fell over. His mother started to panic and was in danger of squashing him. But in seconds three of the grooms moved a partition and helped the foal back to his feet.

We finally landed at Stewart airport, in upstate New York, in early afternoon US time. Sandra and I unloaded our charges, who were a little stiff from having stood still for so long, and put them on the horseboxes for the short drive to quarantine.

And that was all we could do for them. They would be out of our control except, hopefully, when we could lead them out for exercise the following day.

Sandra and I were driven to a motel about five miles away, where we were to stay until the horses could be released.

The next day I rang the quarantine station to find out what time we could exercise them.

'Oh, you can't do that,' twanged the voice down the line.

Further explanations from me about the horses competing in three days' time produced no breakthrough. I had a feeling I was not speaking to the most helpful person.

So I rang Lucinda and David, who, with Clissy, were already at Chesterland. David was acting as our chef d'équipe and I thought he might carry more authority. Ten minutes later David rang me back, saying we could go over to the station that afternoon to walk them out.

Dressed in green overalls and oversized galoshes that made me look ridiculous, Sandra and I waited in a small paddock for the horses to be brought to us.

Both horses looked very bright. The twenty-four hours they had already spent in quarantine had given them time to sleep off their fatigue from the journey, and Gossip was in very good humour. It was the first time he had been looked after by total strangers since 1976, but he did not look the least bit upset or miserable. From his jaunty attitude, I wondered if he had been making fun of the quarantine staff with a show of aggressive behaviour, hoping to frighten them. They had left his headcollar on, which was dusty from the shavings bed and the noseband was covered in the remains of his meals, which seemed to consist, sensibly, mostly of bran. Gossip himself was filthy. His coat was a sticky mess of dried sweat from the journey, and the residue of a powerful-smelling disinfectant that all the animals were washed with when they first came into the station. But despite outer appearances, both horses were in very good form and looked strong and well.

I led Gossip in hand for twenty minutes or so, to stretch and loosen his muscles, and then let him jog a few large circles on the lunge, allowing him to buck and kick if he wanted. At one point, I tripped over one of my outsize galoshes and dropped the lead rope. I snatched back the end before Gossip realised he was loose, which might have stopped any chances of exercise for anyone.

The quarantine staff were kind and let us have them out for nearly threequarters of an hour. Ideally, it would have been better for the horses to have had two short stints of exercise, but that would not have been possible and any time out was better than none at all.

After our compulsory shower we dressed and returned to the motel. There was little else to do but watch endless television, but at least we had the chance to recover from our jet-lag.

On Wednesday morning I again rang the quarantine station, hopeful the horses would be released by lunchtime. The vets' inspection was only thirty hours away; neither horse had been schooled or worked properly since Sunday, and they had to do an FEI test on Friday.

But I received no positive assurances, was refused permission to exercise them, and even David's influence could do nothing. They suggested instead I rang again at lunchtime, which I did and was told the welcome news that the horses could leave at 4 pm, but no, we could not lead them out beforehand.

Gossip and Kingfisher looked very fresh and short of exercise when they were led into a covered area to be signed out by a vet. Gossip fidgeted in circles when I dressed him, stretching his limbs with some well-aimed cow-kicks, after his enforced two days' rest.

It was a six-hour drive south to Chesterland, which was situated 45 minutes west of Philadelphia. As Sandra and I had to travel in the back of the horsebox with Gossip and Kingfisher, I strapped Gossip's hobbles onto his hind legs so that we could have some peace.

It was after 11 pm when the horsebox scrunched up the driveway at Chesterland. It was a warm night, and noisy from the ceaseless clatter of crickets' wings.

A single light blazed from a naked bulb, high up on a barn wall. Below it stood the doors to two empty stables, and I found a note pinned to the stable assigned to Gossip. It read, 'Vets' inspection 8 am.' 'Good grief,' I exclaimed to Sandra, 'surely not the proper one?' Gossip was going to need a thorough shampoo and brush up before he could appear in public. Then, on closer inspection, I discovered it was only the competition vet wanting to check the horses' passports. I hoped he wouldn't mind too much if Gossip looked and smelt as though he hadn't been cleaned for a month.

By the time we had unloaded them a helpful official, who had waited up for us, appeared, and I found more notes from Jane Cobb, Bruce's English groom, telling us where to find hay and feed, as we had not been allowed to import any fodder from England.

Gossip added another layer of dust to his coat as he sat down and rolled in his new lodgings. He was tired but not too irritable; I was sure he would feel fine by the morning. I left him with a small feed and hay, and the kindly official showed Sandra and me to our sleeping quarters, a very smartly furnished caravan parked next to the stables.

The next morning we were up early enough to make Gossip and Kingfisher tidy for their passport checks, and soon after that the riders and their 'chef' arrived. Lucinda and Clissy took the boys for a hack, both horses jiggling and jogging with suppressed energy. Gossip and Kingfisher were very tough individuals mentally and physically; thus they had the perfect constitution to cope with lengthy travel and still come out fighting fit, without any loss of condition.

Lucinda and Clissy almost missed the official vets' inspection that afternoon, through being in the wrong place at the wrong time. Our chef d'équipe had a moment of panic when his first venture into the officialdom of eventing seemed about to end in disaster before it had barely begun.

Gossip was drawn quite near the end of the field in Friday's dressage, so Lucinda gave him two short schooling sessions before his test. Despite the lack of work at the beginning of the week, the eighty-degree temperatures had a soporific effect on high spirits, and Gossip kept his under control to collect a mark of 53.8, which put him into sixth place behind the leader, Karen Stives and Silent Partner on 46 points. Clissy did well to come fourth with 49.

The course, which circumvented the fields around the rolling country of Chesterland, was not quite as demanding as it had been the previous year, but there were still several fences that required the skill of an experienced eye.

The start of phase A was fifteen minutes' walk from where Gossip and Kingfisher were stabled. We had been allotted the permanent boxes this year, as Gossip would have demolished the temporary ones Foxy had used, in seconds.

Knowing how impossible Gossip could be, we allowed 45 minutes from leaving the stables to him starting on phase A.

I led Gossip from a lunge rein attached to his bit, which gave me a few more feet of line to pay out if he tried to nap, whilst Lucinda and David drove slowly behind us in the car, Lucinda waving her jumping whip out of the window whenever Gossip looked like digging his toes in, which he did every hundred yards or so. I had to be careful not to tug on his mouth, which would have made him pull back violently.

Safely at the start, the weighing preliminaries over, we re-saddled him. David held the front end whilst Lucinda and I ducked and dodged the flying hooves as we buckled up the breastplate and tightened the girths, before Gossip's wriggling could dislodge the saddle. Between cow-kicks, I dived under his tummy to do up the overgirth, whose buckle had to be positioned so it would not interfere with horse or rider.

When Lucinda was mounted, I led Gossip in circles in front of the start flags, knowing it would be easier to walk him *back* to the start than to try and bring him *up* to it. As we walked I began to disengage the lunge line from the bit rings.

'Ten seconds,' called the steward. The lunge rein was still in a double loop round one ring.

'Five. . . four. . . three. . . ' A knot in the rein had become snarled on the bit.

'Two. . . one. . .' I feverishly yanked at the rein. It jerked free and wound round my ankles tripping me up. I grabbed at the flags lining the start and Gossip twisted himself round beside me.

'Go!' What luck, we were facing in the right direction. Gossip bounded forward onto phase A. I ran to the car and hurled the lunge rein into the boot in disgust. It would be the shorter, smooth leather lead rein for the other starts.

On our way to the steeplechase, David and I stopped by one of the cross-country fences, a combination, sited near the road; Lucinda wanted to know how other riders were tackling it. This pause caused us to be late at the steeplechase, and as David and I puffed our way over the rise, arms full of buckets and the spare saddle, we could see Gossip already waiting in the start box of phase B. I was amazed that Lucinda had been able to coax him into it without a lead, but the quiet, relaxed atmosphere up at the steeplechase, where there were no spectators or even loudspeakers, had given Gossip no reason to become overexcited and nap. In fact, it was so peaceful that it was hard to believe it was part of the competition. Gossip clearly didn't think it was, as he was standing almost asleep, resting a hind leg.

Lucinda signalled to us that she did not need any assistance, and she kept Gossip in his relaxed position until the countdown reached 'Three. . .' Then she picked up the reins and Gossip swung round to face the start, and was plunging forward as the word 'Go' rang out.

Gossip, with his remarkable acceleration, galloped round the 'chase as though in a race, then he slowed to a trot after the finish, jogged past us waiting at the checkpoint, and disappeared into the trees on the first part of phase C.

David and I wasted no time in returning to the Box before phase D. We could not risk being late there. In the Box were packs of ice-cubes, stacked in polythene bags, laid on by the organisers for the use of any of the competitors to help cool down their horses. I added half a bagful to Gossip's washdown bucket, to keep the water refreshingly cold.

Gossip needed me and the start rein at the beginning of phase D. We were now back at the core of action, amidst a sea of tense nerves and bustling people, with loudspeakers constantly crackling in the background. Gossip was very strong but he did not nap, and the leather rein slipped easily out of the bit rings on the word 'Go'.

There was no close-circuit TV so we had to rely on the commentator. According to him, Gossip was jumping well and moving on very quickly; soon he was on the homeward loop.

The fourth fence from home was at the top of a hill in the field next to Bruce's stable yard. It was a big parallel but its significance lay in the fact that it was only about 75 yards from Gossip's stable.

Gossip flew over the parallel and Lucinda turned him left, away from the stables, and down the steep hill to the water complex. A second later something clicked in Gossip's head; 'Wait a minute, I've seen a short cut.' He slammed on the brakes and tried to whip round on his back legs. Lucinda, nearly falling off at the incredible suddenness of his nap, at first just giggled: it was *so* typical of Gossip. But then matters went beyond a joke when Gossip flatly refused to take another step forward, but reared and napped at a precarious angle on the side of the hill, completely disregarding all Lucinda's efforts at persuasion. He kept this up for over twenty seconds, which seemed like an age. I could see him from where I was standing at the finish, and I really thought he was going to eliminate himself.

Then, as suddenly as he had stopped, he started again. He cantered on down the hill and over the last three fences to finish. He must have decided that maybe Lucinda wasn't going to let him go home early.

Unbelievably he was still within the time, and at the end of the day, he was tied in the lead with Grant Scheidman on the heavily built Flying Dutchman.

This time he really could pull it off, or at least share the victory. But Gossip, being Gossip, would keep everyone on tenterhooks to the last.

After the formality of the vets' inspection in the morning, a friendly crowd of spectators gathered in the field above the stables where the show-jumping was to be held. The informal surroundings lent an almost picnic atmosphere to the occasion.

When Gossip's turn came, he decided to be business-like and professional, and he jumped a clear round. So did Flying Dutchman. The judges dug out a few other comparisons to try and split them. They decided the winner would be the horse nearest the optimum time on the cross country. It wasn't Gossip – despite his unscheduled pause on the hill, he had still been too fast. If only he had napped just another ten seconds longer. . .

The next day Gossip and Kingfisher, who had finished third, flew back to England and their winter holiday.

Chesterland was the sixth time Gossip had been placed second in a three-day event. In itself that was quite a record, but I felt any hopes of Gossip filling the premier spot were as far away as ever, having come so close to two such golden opportunities this year. In 1983 he would be fifteen, an age when many event horses were nearing, or were already in, retirement. Yet Gossip showed no sign of age or disenchantment with eventing. For him there was no other life.

12   Always the Bridesmaid

At the beginning of 1983, we had a change of sponsor: OCL were bowing out after five years of generous and unobtrusive support. The new sponsors, SR Direct Mail (now SR International) headed by John Burbidge, already owned two of the horses at Appleshaw: Shannagh, an intermediate eventer from Ireland, and Super Salesman, who had been show-jumped successfully to Grade B standard. 1982 had been a worrying year for Lucinda and David, as, until early autumn, no one had shown any interest in taking over from OCL. Then SRDM came onto the scene and everyone breathed a lot easier.

One of the first additions SRDM bought was a very smart six-horsebox designed by Huttons of Leicestershire to Lucinda and David's specifications. We had often taken six horses to events, but always had to borrow some form of extra transport. This new pantechnicon would make life at competitions less chaotic and it had a luxurious bonus of living quarters.

Lucinda did not even contemplate entering Gossip for Badminton this year. Ponch and Biggles were on the crest of a wave in their careers and it was only right that they should take precedence.

Gossip was entered for Punchestown again. The course there was big enough to challenge his abilities, and it also meant he didn't have to come back to work until February.

Gossip, being a hot-blooded thoroughbred, thrived on a short, progressive fitness programme before a three-day event. He was usually fully fit in twelve to fourteen weeks, whereas most event horses need fifteen to eighteen weeks, especially if they are starting from scratch after a long winter holiday. If

Gossip was in work for any longer, he quickly became bored and there was the danger of him going 'over the top'.

The problem in dealing with equine athletes is how to keep them fresh mentally. A horse does not have the understanding or self-discipline of the human athlete, so if he finds his work boring and monotonous he will switch off; the result will be only an average performance. The stimulation of competition will help keep interest, but with complex fittening programmes and the caution needed to minimise wear and tear on tendons, which bear the brunt of the galloping and jumping across country, this avenue has its limitations.

A three-day-event horse, once he has attained peak fitness, will only stay mentally and physically at such a level for two to three weeks at the most. The demands made upon him in fast work, combined with the discipline required for a high level of dressage, equate the event horse to the highly tuned engine of a racing car, and just as fickle to maintain.

So in 1983 Gossip started work on St Valentine's Day. It was like riding a Thelwell pony on stilts, he was so round and hairy. Gossip was thrilled to be working again, and he jogged and snatched at the reins as I took him on the road for his first walk. We arrived back in the yard in a steaming mess, meaning I would have to find the clippers and give him an immediate haircut before he lost too much weight through sweating.

After a cross-country school near the end of March, Lucinda entered him in the advanced class at Rushall, knowing how little he bothered over smaller courses. It wasn't a very successful outing. Gossip scraped his stifles when he left a leg behind, jumping up a sleeper bank over a stream, and Shannagh showed his inexperience by trying to clear the log and the bank all in one go, where a bounce was needed, and turned a somersault. Shannagh and Lucinda finished the course with no apparent injuries, but Shannagh pulled up at the end with one hind leg covered in blood, although he wasn't lame or sore. Washing the leg, I discovered a tiny cut just below his stifle where he must have nicked a small vein.

The timing of Rushall's dates were perfect, as the event was held the weekend before Badminton. This meant that Gossip could have a lazy week to recover from his Rushall exertions and be none the wiser as to what his colleagues were up to in Gloucestershire.

I don't really like to think I believe in fairy tales. When Lucinda, David, myself and Gig Lees, who was looking after Mairangi for David, left for Badminton, it never seriously entered my head that we'd be in for another fantastically magical moment like the one we'd had last September in Luhmühlen.

The idea that Ponch could win Badminton wasn't exactly unthinkable to most people; in fact, he was one of the favourites. But to those who knew him and the difficulties of producing any sort of dressage test that could keep him in touch with the top twenty horses, the feat was as unexpected and exciting as it had been only months before in Germany.

We had a nerve-racking Saturday night at Badminton, when Ponch was found to be very sore from a bruised heel. Since he had so nearly fallen two years ago in Boekelo, when one of his front feet had trodden on the opposite over-reach boot, we had stopped using that piece of tack. We felt, anyway, that the thin rubber did not afford a great deal of protection.

It was a gamble, and maybe a wrong one. The night was broken up by strapping bags of crushed ice to Ponch's bruised heel, interspersed by two-minute treatments of Ultrasound in the expert hands of our vet, Paul, who had driven over late that evening in response to a plea from Lucinda.

By 6 am Ponch was sound, but Paul was concerned that if he knocked the heel again it would aggravate the soreness. Once we were safely through the vets' inspection on Sunday morning, Paul neatly bandaged the heel to protect it during the show-jumping that afternoon.

A few hours later, Ponch posed for photos outside the Whitbread Tent, with Lucinda beside him holding the Whitbread Trophy. It was her fifth win; she had beaten the record of four Badminton victories set by Mark Phillips.

John Burbidge of SRDM couldn't stop beaming. A shrewd businessman, it nevertheless was a risk to put up sponsorship, and it was quite remarkable to be paid back so quickly with such a prestigious win. In fact, Lucinda and David had had a fantastic run of success that spring, with one or the other winning a class at virtually every event we attended.

David's luck maliciously deserted him at Badminton. Approaching the hayracks, the third to last fence, and still clear, he looked set to take the lead. Mairangi cleared the first element, then at the second he veered sharply left. David pulled him back on line but the abruptness of the movement projected David out of the saddle. They jumped the third part together, but with David hanging on beside Mairangi, facing his tail. The entire spectacle was an extraordinary display of acrobatics, and Gig and I watching on the close-circuit TV in the Box couldn't quite believe what we were seeing. Neither horse nor rider was injured, but the sixty penalties for a fall ruthlessly pushed them down the ratings.

There was no break in the hectic pace of life at Appleshaw after Badminton. The evening we returned, the horsebox was unloaded and cleaned out ready for 'business as usual' the next morning. Six of the other event horses were badly in need of fitness work and would have to be boxed to their work-out area.

Celebratory bubbles of champagne rapidly fizzed out of the system as we tacked up horses at 7 am the next morning. Whilst I was feeling somewhat jaded, despite the exhilaration of winning, Gossip was in wickedly top form, and I had to grit my teeth and control my patience as he fidgeted and cow-kicked with anticipation while I tacked him up for Lucinda. 'Thank goodness it isn't me riding you,' I said to him, as he stuck his tongue over his bit and waggled it at me, a habit he insisted on as soon as the bit was put in his mouth.

I informed Lucinda that Village Gossip was in spanking form, and she rolled her eyes heavenwards knowing that meant he would behave abominably on the hills, plunging and pulling and refusing to leave the others.

Bicton was the next event on Gossip's calendar and so, it seemed, was the local monsoon. It started raining at 7 am and did not let up until the evening. The warm-up area for the show-jumping became an ankle-deep morass of mud, the consistency of pea soup.

Gossip, never at his best in the wet, sulked in the dressage, crabbing away from the driving rain. He slithered round the show-jumping, but did cheer up considerably as he jogged up to the start of the cross country. He finished the course clear and I led him back to the horsebox, checking him over as I went, for signs of injuries. As we crossed a tarmac road I noticed his feet sounded muffled. I stopped and picked up each front foot in turn. Both shoes were missing. Lucinda had not felt anything wrong on the course, and we concluded that he must have pulled them off in the gluey base of the water jump, which was the penultimate fence.

As a precaution against possible bruising, we poulticed both front feet, and a very embarrassed Gossip shuffled down the ramp back at Appleshaw, his feet encased in sacking and polythene. He looked like an old man in well-worn bedroom slippers. His tough little feet showed no sign of soreness, however, and he was re-shod the next day.

David's ride for Punchestown was the impressive Walk-about, who had been sweeping the board in intermediates and open intermediates that spring.

Gossip was in superb shape at Punchestown and looked stronger than he had done the previous year, with much less of a wasp waist, as he had not needed to be in work for so long.

Ireland lived up to its reputation as a rain-swept isle. The weather was cold, with showers of icy lashing rain.

The sodden turf in the dressage area became heavier and muddier as each competitor followed in the tracks of his predecessor. In this situation it can be difficult for the rider to decide whether to ride accurately and stay in the mud churned up by the other horses, which will hamper their own horse's movement, or to move in off the track, giving the horse a better chance to show his paces but losing a few marks through being slightly inaccurate.

Lucinda kept Gossip out of the mud, which he detested, and was rewarded with an obedient flowing test and a mark of 52, that left them in second place to Irish rider Gerry Sinnot on The Prop. David was thrilled with the often ebullient Walkabout, who looked very assured, and went into seventh place.

Lucinda kept her foot firmly on the accelerator this time, and Gossip's superiority across country was unchallenged.

Almost unbelievably, he was back in the position he had occupied twelve months ago: he was leading the field, but this time with two fences in hand from another Irish rider, Gillian Kyle on Santex. David's accursed gremlin of misfortune had dogged him again. Walkabout's fast, confident clear on the cross country had pulled them up to third, but on the scoreboard beside their names was a large 'E' for Elimination. Apparently, David had missed a turning flag on the course. David was almost certain he had made no such error, but the judge's word is final unless the case can be proved otherwise, and the infuriating decision had to stand.

Two fences in hand. This time Gossip's elusive victory seemed assured. It was rare for him to knock down more than that. He changed that record soon enough, and hit five. Poor, poor Gossip. He had genuinely tried his best to clear each fence, but he desperately needed firm ground as a springboard. The sponginess of the Punchestown arena offered him no help at all, and he could not quite tuck up his hooves out of danger. For the sixth time in an international three-day event, he had to play bridesmaid. This time to Santex, who had achieved a very careful clear round and well deserved the trophy that he won.

For some reason, I was not so disappointed that Gossip hadn't won. As he entered the show-jumping arena, I had a feeling he wasn't going to win. The previous year, the vibes, or whatever it is one feels when things are going well, were there and the atmosphere felt positive. And in the end, the winner was the right one. Botany Bay had given nothing less than his best, and was justly victorious for his efforts. This year Gossip genuinely had not put a foot wrong and it seemed a little unfair that he was not blessed with a little of the 'luck of the Irish'. But an event horse has to operate in all types of going. Winning a three-day event is never, ever easy and riders and horses have to cope with the conditions as they arise.

Santex had also been foot-perfect throughout the event but had coped more comfortably with the going. On the day that mattered, he was the better horse.

In dramatic contrast to rain-soaked Ireland, I found myself on a plane a few days later, with Shannagh, en route to the sunny climes of Kentucky and the site of those '78 World Championships. The Americans had since then used Lexington for their major three-day event of the spring season, but with the fences drastically modified and the notorious Serpent removed from the course altogether. Shannagh had now progressed to advanced standard, helped by a seventh place at Boekelo the previous autumn, and it was anticipated that the altered Lexington course would suit him well.

I had an anxious time in quarantine when one of the French event horses which had flown out with us for the competition, showed a positive result on one of his blood tests. This very nearly caused Shannagh and me to be returned to England as there was the risk of infection, the two horses having been on the same plane. Argumentative telephone calls between the organisers at Lexington and the quarantine station ensued, whilst Lucinda, waiting in Lexington, kept me abreast of what was going on. This state of affairs continued for four days and in that time I was allowed to lead Shannagh out twice, which in itself was quite something because the French horses were not allowed out at all from their quarantine stables.

Eventually the authorities relented and Shannagh was released to continue his journey to Kentucky, but the luckless French horses were flown back to Europe.

On Monday morning Shannagh and I were collected by a hired horsebox for the fifteen-hour drive to Kentucky. We arrived at the stables at Lexington at three in the morning, and Shannagh was so tired he spent the next twelve hours lying down, apart from mealtimes. In twenty-four hours he was his normal self, but the dressage day was almost upon us and he had not been schooled for a week.

As it happened, torrential rain on the morning of the test prevented any horse from showing its best, as they splashed through the sand arena which had almost disappeared under water.

On cross-country day blue skies and soaring temperatures called for ice in the Box to help cool the horses as they finished, and care had to be taken to avoid the risk of sun-blistered backs from drying sweat. The course was well built, extremely jumpable and the time generous. Shannagh seemed oblivious to the heat and finished clear, inside the time, without any signs of distress. The Americans had done their homework well, learning from the aftermath of 1978.

On Sunday, Shannagh jumped a stylish clear round and finished eighth, the higher placings going to top-flight American event horses.

Shannagh had been rather more in the limelight over the earlier part of the week, when Rolex, the famous watch-makers, had photographed him and Lucinda as advertisements for their products. Shannagh was a perfect model, standing quietly wherever he was put, and pricking his ears as the shutter clicked. A great deal more co-operative than a certain other gentleman I know, I mused, thinking how Gossip would have pulled terrible faces, tried to kick the cameraman or, even worse, scrunched up a valuable watch.

Shannagh and I arrived back at Heathrow two days after Lexington finished, to be greeted by Gig, who had driven up to meet us with the horsebox but with the unwelcome news that our tackroom had been burgled the previous night. What luck that I had all Lucinda's tack with me and that the thieves had failed to locate David's, which was kept elsewhere. It was a nasty shock, though, and we have since taken strong measures against a reoccurrence.

Gossip looked as sleek as a well-fed seal when he came back into work in early July. His programme for the autumn was to culminate in the three-day event at Boekelo in October.

Before then there was an overflowing schedule of events to be fitted into August and September, one of the first being the new prestigious Croft Original One Day Championships at Gatcombe Park, home of H.R.H. Princess Anne and Capt. Mark Phillips. The event had attracted much publicity beforehand and a mass of spectators descended on the estate, many, I thought, more eager for a glimpse of the house and grounds, and, more importantly, the occupants, than the competition.

David might have had ill-luck at three-day events but he

was a dangerous rival in one-days, and at the end of the competition at Gatcombe, he and Lucinda lay equal first on Mairangi and Beagle Bay. To split them, the judges had to refer back to the dressage marks before they were evened up by the multiplying factor, and Mairangi came out just ahead.

Mairaingi's win was a very special one. The standard of competition at Gatcombe was comparable to a high-class three-day event and had included several European riders chasing the generous prize-money. It was a just reward for this highly talented horse who, like Gossip, had never claimed a major prize. It was aptly timed too, as Mairangi was retired from eventing that autumn. His jumping ability was put to use in the hunting field, and Mairangi was in his element as he followed hounds. Sadly, in the winter of '85 his legs were unable to keep up with his body's demands and the kindest solution was to let him go, as the Indians say, to 'the happy hunting grounds in the sky'.

Much of August was taken up with the European Championships in Frauenfeld, Switzerland. Lucinda and Ponch were once again in the team. This time the Brits had to concede first place to the Swedes in the team competition. However, Rachel Bayliss achieved a great personal victory in the individual, on Mystic Minstrel, and Ponch caught up after his average dressage to take the individual silver.

The week after Frauenfeld I found myself up at Springhill open intermediate, coping with a revved-up Gossip who was bursting to return to the fray. He hurtled round the course in flippant fashion and came into third place. He then had to sit and drum his heels for three weeks until his next event.

In the interim, Shannagh and Super Salesman for David, competed at Burghley. Super Salesman, or Sam, as he is known, came to Appleshaw the previous autumn, having never seen a cross-country course. He started his eventing career at Crookham the following spring in the novice class, and six months later was looking more than ready to take on Burghley, having easily upgraded to advanced.

The week of Burghley was blasted by cold winds and squally showers, reminding us that autumn was only round the corner. Sam, indifferent to the conditions, went like a dream, finding the whole competition effortless, and finished in eighth place. Shannagh did not find the course anything like as easy and collected faults for two refusals when he became confused during his approaches. He is not as quick-thinking as Gossip or Ponch, and Lucinda realised that his education would have to be taken at a steadier pace.

Three days after Burghley, I was extremely lucky (though having to dig deep into my reserves of energy) to fly once again across the Atlantic to Chesterland. This time Lucinda was riding Biggles and we were accompanied by Walkabout, who was cared for by Australian Emma D'Arcy, who was now looking after David's horses.

Meanwhile, back at Appleshaw Gossip was putting on his most unco-operative act for Lorna Knox, my aide-de-campe, who was in charge of him at Tetbury Horse Trials. Whenever an opportunity presented itself, he napped. He kicked and bucked when Lorna changed saddles and washed him down, and lastly, he flatly refused to pick up either hind foot for Lorna to remove the jumping studs. He had even collected a stop on the cross country at an insignificant fence, but Lucinda admitted this was her fault for over-controlling him.

Chesterland's course was little changed and Biggles cruised round after one of his best ever tests to take the lead after the cross country. But in the show-jumping he completely demolished the first part of the last treble, and was incredibly lucky to amass only four faults. But those few faults were expensive and he slid down to fourth. Walkabout consolidated his potential; clear rounds in the cross country and show-jumping put him fifth place.

Back from the States, we had only a week before repacking the trunks and loading up the horsebox for the trip to Boekelo, the final event of the year. Gossip was at last content that he now had my undivided attention.

David was riding Fair Deal, nicknamed Savage because he pulled the most frightening faces – there was no malice intended but his expressions could be extremely off-putting.

Boekelo is very much a fun event with an end-of-term atmosphere that sets it aside from the other three-day events on the international calendar. Nevertheless, it is still quite an important event to win and is popular amongst competitors. The Dutch organisers work hard to ensure a smoothly run competition; this, combined with generous hospitality in the form of drinks or supper parties nearly every night, means that Boekelo is guaranteed, weather permitting, to be a success.

And by some miracle the weather did stay dry the entire week. Emma must have thought me mad as I had warned her that we usually spent most of the event dressed in macs and wellies. This year not a drop of rain fell and the sun kept the autumn fogs at bay.

Through the week, Gossip was his normal obnoxious self, his high level of fitness bringing about an equally high level of kicking and bucking whenever I groomed him. If he hadn't behaved in his usual impossible manner I would have been worried that he was ill.

One afternoon Charles Harrison, the chef d'équipe, was trying to hold a riders' briefing to discuss the course, just outside the tented stabling but only a few yards from Gossip's stable, wherein I was attempting to groom. The rattle and crash of his hooves thwarted all concentration and the meeting had to be moved out of earshot.

The marks were very close after the dressage: Gossip was lying eighteenth on 52.4, but only five points behind the leader; Savage was forty-first and only seven marks behind Gossip.

The steeplechase at Boekelo could only be reached by using one of the mini-buses laid on by the organisers. These ran a shuttle service to and from the stables all day. Though fairly reliable there was always the slight risk you could mis-time your arrival at one end or the other.

However, with Gossip it was imperative that I be ready for him at the start of the steeplechase in case he tried to nap. So after a perfectly timed start to phase A I scrambled into an already overloaded bus and trundled off towards phase B. It stopped by the gateway to the steeplechase field and I could see the start several hundred yards away. The steeplechase course at Boekelo runs part way round the perimeter of a lake then doubles back on itself. One year someone mounted a video camera on a speed-boat and tried to film the action from the lake, but this unnerved the horses so much that their concentration lapsed from the fences, and the filming had to be stopped.

I arrived in time to start Gossip, who anyway ignored me and stared out across the lake as we waited for the off. As the countdown ended, Gossip swung towards me as he spun round to head out of the start box, and I slipped the rein and ducked out of his way in one fluid movement. With no boats or windsurfers to ogle at on the lake Gossip thought about what he was doing and was soon through the finish and jogging down phase C.

I hurried back to the road, scanning the area for a mini-bus. Nothing in sight. Then I saw one coming my way, bursting with people, most of them spectators. It stopped beside me and a few people alighted. I squeezed my way on board. Then, to my amazement, the driver turned off the engine, mumbled something in Dutch and hopped out of his seat. Another mini-bus pulled up alongside and I watched as that driver deserted his passengers too, and the two of them began lighting cigarettes and unwrapping breadrolls for a snack lunch.

With me was one of the parents of another British rider, also in a hurry to return to base. Between us we managed to make one of the drivers understand that maybe his lunch could wait a while, and at last we were bouncing along the track back to the stables.

We reached the Box in plenty of time, and I felt rather guilty at having chivvied the driver.

Out on the cross country Gossip was clear and within the time. But so were many others. Over the years the time allowed had been eased, and if a rider did not hang about, it was perfectly possible to finish inside it. Gossip climbed up into fifth place, and Savage, emulating Gossip's round, shot into seventh.

The next day Gossip jumped clear and moved up another two places, but Savage had one fence down and he dropped right down to fourteenth.

That night the good weather broke and for the next three

days we were marooned in Holland. Strong winds and rain battered the coastline making the seas far too rough to ferry the horses.

As all the Continental horses had left, David moved some partitions in the empty stables to give Gossip and Savage more room. At one end of the tent, workmen had already begun to dismantle the temporary boxes, and we hoped they wouldn't insist on Gossip and Savage moving out.

Emma and I hacked them out each day, and I had to work hard to encourage Gossip's walk out of a disgruntled crawl. He was so fed up at being ridden when he should have been starting his holidays that whenever Savage came within range, he snaked his head and neck out and bit him peevishly on the backside.

On Wednesday morning the wind dropped. Convinced there would be no problems we loaded up the horses at 7 am only to see Lucinda returning from the telephone, shaking her head. It was still blowing hard on the coast, and the wind had to drop before the sea would be calm enough to take horses. Twenty-four hours later we crossed back to England. As we drove across the South Downs towards Hampshire, the leaves were turning red and gold and beginning to drift from the trees. For the next two and half months the pace of life would slow to a dawdle, as horses and riders went into a kind of hibernation until the following spring.

13   *Vintage Year*

1984 was to be the year of the Olympic Games in Los Angeles. With the ever-changing face of politics and world economy, the media were heralding these Games as possibly the last Olympics to uphold true amateurism in sport.

1984 also brought Gossip to school-leaving age. He was sixteen years young and showed no signs of wanting to give up the sport he loved so much. He was fit, sound and as strong as ever; he had lost none of his jumping ability: which is why Lucinda decided to enter him for Badminton.

He had not run over such a testing course since 1981 but the courses he had completed since that time, he had tossed off with justifiable nonchalance. Lucinda was aware he could run at Punchestown again, but there was no reason why he should not be allowed one last chance at Badminton. And Lucinda knew which course would give Gossip more pleasure to tackle.

Certain provisos were set against Gossip running at Badminton. First, if at any time he showed any sign of stress or strain or hinted at his age in the months before, he would be immediately withdrawn. Second, if Badminton week turned out to be one of April showers, transforming the ground into a squelching morass, Gossip would not run. And third, if at any moment while on the course Lucinda felt him tire, or that he wasn't happy and jumping well, then she would pull up.

Gossip's stable runner for Badminton was to be the fourteen-year-old Biggles. Ponch had been permitted by the selectors to by-pass Badminton, as he was already on the short-list for Los Angeles.

Gossip's and Biggles' first foray of the year was in mid-February, to an indoor show-jumping competition at Burley Villa in the New Forest. Three of the younger horses accompanied them, and showed up their elders in no uncertain terms. Whilst the babies picked up placings in almost every class they entered, Gossip and Biggles proceeded to fool about in the practice ring, and then amassed a stack of unnecessary faults as they mischievously tipped rails to the floor. I hoped such antics would be confined to lesser competitions.

A cross-country school at the beginning of March with Lady Hugh, high up on Salisbury Plain amidst flurries of snow, did little to hinder their enthusiasm. Indeed Gossip glowed with good health and well-being.

At long last we had just enough control to attempt interval training with him. Even so, we had to use a complicated set of tack, comprising a bitless bridle with a vulcanite snaffle underneath, and a running martingale. As long as the pace stayed at a steady canter, Gossip remained quite sober. But for any increase in speed, Gossip insisted on going flat out.

This more disciplined work developed his top-line much more successfully than ever before, and he maintained the all-important muscle behind the saddle which built up more easily now he was working in a conventional outline.

Crookham opened the spring season and gave both horses an excellent warm-up, Biggles coming third and Gossip sixth.

Gossip's next event was to be Frensham, but continuous rain on an already soaking ground caused the competition to be cancelled. His alternative was Rushall, where he took the lead after his cross-country round only to be demoted by Ponch, who sneaked home a second or two faster.

On 10th April, Gossip, Biggles, Walkabout and Sam travelled up to Badminton. The four comprised the two oldest and two youngest advanced event horses in the yard, Walkabout and Sam (David's two rides) being only eight years old but possessing the ability and skill of seasoned horses. The ground had dried, and the weather was unusually warm and spring-like, much in Gossip's favour.

Our allocated stables were in the peaceful Portcullis yard, hidden away from the bustle of the main yard where the majority of the horses were billeted. Gossip's stable had a full door, so he could not look out except through the barred window at one end. This arrangement suited him well as he loathed people staring at him and became very bad-tempered if his rest-time was constantly interrupted by a barrage of curious faces.

This year, as Gossip was trotted up for the ground jury at the first vets' inspection, Lucinda sighed with relief that she did not have to send Gossip home. Unless the weather changed there was nothing to stop Gossip attempting his fifth trip around the famous course.

Gossip and Sam were to do their dressage on the Thursday. They were both more difficult to settle in an arena than the other two and there were usually less crowds on the first day.

Throughout his test Gossip behaved like a cool professional. It was hard to believe that this same horse had given Charlie such a miserable time three years earlier. And Gossip's mark joined the ranks of normality, when he gained 63. At last his notorious reputation in the arena had been laid to rest.

David had a less enjoyable time with Sam and it was a monumental achievement that he kept him within the dressage boards. The stocky, powerful grey had become so tense in his tests that he was almost unridable; none of us could understand why he had suddenly changed so. Outsiders may have been surprised at his mark of 99.8, but we were all relieved that Sam had at least not eliminated himself by jumping out of the arena, or lost his rider by rearing at X, as he had earlier that spring.

On Friday, Walkabout performed a good test which put him a few places behind Gossip, and Biggles, though barely able to control his high spirits, headed the field with a lively performance that was also accurate and fluent. We were thrilled he had done so well but at the same time nervous of the pressure it would bring to bear on the crucial cross country to come. Any mistakes would be expensive ones, and there would be nowhere to go but downwards.

Saturday dawned clear and misty, promising one of those rare spring days when you could be forgiven for thinking that summer had arrived early. For Gossip, the ground, weather and conditions were perfect.

Amidst a sea of faces, as crowds thronged at the start of

phase A, I led Gossip around the roped-off area to loosen him up before Lucinda mounted. As always, the atmosphere was electric. As Lorna, who had come up to help me, straightened the day rug, Gossip let out a squeal and a buck, unable to contain his excitement. Years ago he'd have done the same thing out of fury but now he used the excuse as a pressure valve on his pent-up nerves.

Once Lucinda had mounted, I almost had to run to keep up with his walk and to ensure that I kept the lead rein slack so he felt no pressure on his mouth. As the last seconds ticked away we approached the start flags, and Lorna positioned herself behind Gossip lest he should try to nap. Gossip was keen to start, and without any backward glances he bounded through the flags onto phase A.

He was superb on the steeplechase, no longer tearing off in a frenzy, wasting energy by going faster then he needed. He swept through the finish and onto phase C just a second inside the time.

An hour later, I was holding him in the start box of phase D. Gossip, as usual, was facing backwards, his head alert as he listened to the countdown. Lucinda picked up the reins, I let the lead rein slither through the rings as she did so. Gossip spun towards me and away across Badminton Park for the last time.

It was the challenge Gossip had been waiting for for three years, and he showed off all the skill and experience he had acquired in the eight years he had been at the top. He lowered himself so close to the fence into the lake that he scraped his stifles, despite the thick layer of protective grease with which I had covered his legs. At the Pig-sties Lucinda chose the quick route, which involved a short but steep slope to rails followed by a bounce and wide spread. Gossip gave us an anxious moment when he slithered over the spread, and this sight deterred many other riders from taking that same route. At the Quarry a gasp went up when he put in a mighty leap at the wall coming out at the top of the slope. Two and a half minutes later Gossip was cheered home as he jumped the Whitbread Bar and galloped through the finish. He had completed the course clear and within the time.

Leading him back through the seething crowds to the stables, Gossip pulled and jogged. Lorna had to walk in front of us to clear the way before Gossip knocked someone over. He was so pleased with himself, he was all but smiling; Lorna and I grinned from ear to ear, relieved that he had come through unscathed. Back at the stables, we washed him down and checked and bandaged his legs. I left Lorna to apply ice-packs to his stifles in case the lake fence had left any bruising.

Biggles was restlessly pacing his stable in anticipation. He looked extremely scruffy as he had rolled, filling his plaits with shavings, and his rugs were slipping to one side.

An hour later he was bucking in explosive bouts of energy as I led him to the start of phase A.

At 6 pm that evening four tired but contented horses stood munching haynets in their stables at Badminton. Not one of them had put a foot wrong. Piling on the pressure even more, Biggles had retained his lead with a brilliantly fast clear round. Gossip lay seventh and Walkabout thirteenth. Sam had clawed his way up to mid-field, having been bottom after the dressage. They were all in good heart and sound, with no more than a few superficial cuts from the odd scrape and bump.

On Sunday, Walkabout jumped clear and moved up to eleventh. Gossip, suffering no ill-effects or soreness from his stifles, pinged round the course, also clear and going two places higher.

I hardly dared watch Biggles' round. He always rolled a pole somewhere, and I could see no reason why today should be different. Biggles had led right from the start of this year's competition and it seemed too impossible that he could do so all the way through. But he did.

After Badminton until early August, life revolved around Ponch and the Games. In Los Angeles the British team put up a tremendous show but they could not quite overhaul the strong American team, and we had to settle for the silver medal. Ginny Holgate and Priceless captured the individual bronze, and Ponch, performing well but pegged back by his dressage, finished sixth.

In the autumn of 1984, Gossip's first competition was in

Scotland, in the attractive grounds of Thirlstane Castle. The course was beautifully built and reasonably straightforward for an advanced class. It was a suitable opener for Gossip and for Lucinda's other ride, Brass Monkey, who was taking on his first advanced, as was David's little brown Gucci.

Gossip was in top form, and exasperated me to the point where he nearly had a bucket of water thrown at him for the second time in his life. He bucked and squealed in anticipation every time I saddled him up. After the cross country, he was so pleased with himself he couldn't keep still, nor could any of his legs. The sponge and sweat-scraper flew through the air as he jolted them out of my hand. He kicked over the water bucket then slammed his backside against me so that I fell flat on my back. All this was accomplished with the most irritating smirk on his face; it was obvious he knew exactly how much of a nuisance he was being. David came over to sympathise. He grabbed Gossip's nose and half twisted it, as though to twitch him. Gossip's expression was that of a schoolboy being hauled up before the headmaster. And the method worked. Rather than suffer a sore nose, Gossip stood like a rock, eyes rolling in their sockets as he watched David warily on one side and me sloshing water on the other.

But it was a successful trip to Thirlstane. Gucci impressed everyone with a third place, Gossip was fourth, and Brass Monkey, who went more slowly across country, was twelfth.

A month later, the same three went to Gatcombe. Gossip did his dressage on the Saturday, the day before the main part of the event, in a quiet field, watched by only a handful of spectators.

One of his favourite judges, Mrs Allhusen, was presiding. Gossip was in mellow mood and produced a lovely test, using his shoulders and working through from behind more than I'd ever seen before.

On Sunday, he show-jumped clear and then set off on the cross country at his normal bone-rattling pace. The Gatcombe course is like a scaled-down version of a three-day event course, such are the dimensions of the fences.

As Gossip faced up to fence eight, four steps cut into the side of a steep slope, Lucinda half wondered if she should take

(ABOVE) Before the start of Phase A, Badminton 1984. Lucinda attaches her watch and I attach the start rein.

(ABOVE) 'Where's the next?' Gossip at the Lake (Badminton 1984). *Findlay Davidson*
(BELOW) Gossip stepping neatly off the 'Fravenfeld platform', (Badminton ,1984). *Findlay Davidson*

(TOP) In his usual backwards facing position before the start of Phase A. Lucinda ignores the reins until the last few seconds. I prepare to slip the lead rein. David stands ready to lend a hand (Boekelo 1984).
(ABOVE RIGHT) Mum sits tight through a rare mistake. *Michael Reddick*
(ABOVE LEFT) En route to his Gatcombe victory. . . . *Michael Reddick*

(TOP) 'Can I go?' Gossip waits at the start of the 'chase' (Boekelo 1984).

(ABOVE) As keen at sixteen as he was when he was six (Boekelo 1984).

(LEFT) *Clare Lampen*

the easier, slower route, as Gossip, relying on speed more than power, often found steps a bit of a struggle. But Gossip never hesitated and bounced straight up where others put in a shuffly stride.

Gossip practically smiled as he was led back to the horsebox. He was feeling so contented he forgot to be a nuisance. I was even able to wash him down without help.

He had gone so well, Lucinda knew he would be somewhere in the first six. Suddenly a Range Rover bumped up to the lowered side ramp of our horsebox and Mark Phillips wound down his window, urging, 'Quick, Cinders, get in – you've won!'

Lucinda stopped struggling with her stock, and gawped like a surprised fish. 'Eh? You're kidding?' she spluttered through a stock-pin gripped in her teeth.

'Nope,' insisted a grinning Mark. 'Gossip's won by 0.7 of a second. Davey and Andrew Hoy are second; he put in a stride up one of the four steps where Gossip bounced.'

Luck was finally on Gossip's side. The 'if only' belonged to someone else.

14 Onwards and Upwards

Gossip competed at Boekelo that October, and finished fourteenth. Unbeknownst to him, he was carrying two people, the second being young Freddie Green, who showed his face to the world six months later.

After Boekelo, Lucinda was in a quandary. Gossip was approaching his seventeenth birthday. In deference to his age if nothing else, it was time he was retired from three-day eventing. In body and spirit, Gossip was the same as ever. He was sound, still galloped full tilt at everything, and his brain was as sharp-thinking as it had always been. Gossip was one of those horses who would keep going until he dropped.

The problem was, what could Gossip do as an alternative? It would be a refined form of torture to turn him out permanently to grass. Many event horses were retired to the hunting field, but Lucinda was sceptical of that possibility with Gossip. He pulled hard enough on his own, so what would he be like with a large field of followers? (We had no idea then, that he had ever hunted with Katie.) And who would be good enough to hunt him? Lucinda simply did not have the time.

There was only one person that she could envisage would be able to cope with Gossip in the hunting field – Joss Hanbury. Joss was Joint Master of the Cottesmore and Quorn Hunts and a superb horseman. He was an old friend of Lucinda's and he lived in the peaceful magnificence of his inheritance, Burley-on-the-Hill, in the now extinct county of Rutland, with wife Rozzy and their three small children.

Joss had hunted Be Fair for a while and had helped bring on several young event horses that Lucinda had sent him over the years, sharpening them up in the rough and tumble of the hunting field. Joss had also hunted some of the more experienced eventers who needed freshening up before returning to the event circuit. Shannagh had benefited enormously from a short season's hunting the previous winter, and had won Punchestown the following May in positive and determined style.

So after a two-week holiday to recover from Boekelo, Gossip was sent north in company with two younger novices.

Whilst Lucinda was worrying over Gossip's performance in the hunting field, I was far more concerned at how anyone was going to look after him. Gossip's behaviour in the stable hardly endeared him to people, so how were the grooms at Burley-on-the-Hill to interpret his threats? Even more upsetting, if Gossip found that nobody trusted him, would he degenerate into the miserable suspicious horse that we and the Brookeboroughs had encountered so many years ago? Lucinda was also acutely conscious that this might happen and she assured me that if Gossip was not enjoying life up there, she would bring him back to Appleshaw immediately.

Our fears were unfounded. Within days of arriving at Burley-on-the-Hill, Gossip had settled in and was almost hero-worshipped by Joss's two girl grooms. They adored him so much that they gave each other photos of Gossip for Christmas.

Lucinda had warned Joss of Gossip's numerous idiosyncrasies, to the extent that Joss and the girls initially approached Gossip very gingerly, not quite sure what to expect. But Gossip sensed that they were 'honest injuns' and not out to get him, and the cautious barriers between them were soon broken down.

The first time Joss took Gossip hunting, Joss confessed to being extremely nervous at the prospect of the unknown. Joss chose an unimportant meet, over not very inspiring country, to test out his new hunter.

To begin with, all went well, Gossip behaving admirably and boosting Joss's confidence. Soon hounds picked up a scent and the field followed, galloping down the wide grass verges bordering the roads. Suddenly hounds checked. The fox had done a complete U-turn and doubled back. The field pulled up and parted to make way for Joss to come through and lead them back up the road. Gossip wouldn't turn round. He stood in the middle of the road and reared, as he had done countless times over the years whenever he disagreed with a change of plan.

While Joss and Gossip argued, the rest of the field quietly went on ahead leaving them to it. Eventually Joss had to give in. He dismounted and led Gossip back up the road. As he rejoined everyone else, friends exclaimed 'Gosh, that's a very green horse you have there, Joss.'

The rest of the day passed without incident, but it left Joss with some niggling doubts in his mind as to how they would cope with a bigger field on a good scenting day. Napping was one of Gossip's little quirks Lucinda hadn't mentioned.

Lucinda had instructed Joss that Gossip must be ridden fast into all his fences because he relied on his speed to clear them and hated to be dictated to. Joss couldn't believe this applied to absolutely every fence. So when, on about his third day out with Gossip, they headed towards a small set of posts and rails, Joss kept Gossip at a slow hand-canter. Gossip made a complete hash of the fence, somehow paddling through it, and it was pure luck that they both ended up in one piece on the landing side. Joss was amazed that Gossip had made such a muddle over such a simple fence, but he made a mental note to heed Lucinda's advice thereafter.

The only time Gossip and Joss did come to grief and hit the ground, a fence wasn't even involved. They were galloping across a field towards a wide-open gateway. Although Joss could control Gossip's pace, it was quite a tussle, so unless a slower speed was strictly necessary, Joss tended to let Gossip gallop, knowing the horse was clever enough to keep out of trouble. Joss didn't give the gateway a second thought as they galloped through. Next minute he found himself face down in mud, Gossip struggling to his feet beside him. Gossip had galloped straight into a large tractor-tyre rut hidden under a puddle in the gateway, and had turned a complete somersault. The two of them rose from the mire, quite unrecognisable. Joss had to wipe the mud from his eyes in order to see, and

Gossip kept shaking his head trying to dislodge water from his ears.

Poor Gossip, at Lexington he had suffered a mud bath at the Serpent. Then at Locko in '81 he had again been submerged. But this was the final insult; he hadn't even had to leave the ground. Joss found Gossip to be in a very angry, disgruntled mood for the rest of the day.

Another day, Gossip took the law into his own hands. The field was spread out across a grass meadow and was approaching a solid-looking hedge and ditch. Joss, always looking to take the quickest route, was heading for a particularly hair-raising part. Gossip sized up the situation in seconds. He took one look at what was in front of him, and veered away towards an easier spot where other people were jumping. When hounds checked, Joss was congratulated on wisely jumping his young horse over a simple part of the fence-line.

Nobody ever recognised Gossip out hunting, assuming he was an insignificant young horse. Certainly word had spread that Joss had the famous Village Gossip to hunt, but whenever Joss appeared on Gossip, nobody took any notice. Yet when Joss rode a more substantial hunter, people enquired politely if that was the great Gossip. They could not believe that the slightly built, 16 hh dark-brown gelding was the international event horse.

Joss was cautious as to the amount of times Gossip hunted and restricted his outings to three times a fortnight. He always took Gossip as first horse, feeling Gossip would be impossible if he had to wait for the changeover to second horses in the early afternoon. Surprisingly, Gossip was remarkably well mannered and never tried to kick at meets or in crowded gateways.

But just before Christmas, Gossip went lame when one of his front joints showed signs of wear. In January, Gossip returned to Appleshaw and enjoyed a long spring holiday.

On the first of May I tacked him up and took him out for his half-hour's walk round the roads, in preparation for possibly a few one-day events later on. Gossip, far from feeling idle as he often did on the first few days of work, strode energetically along the road, pausing only to snatch at clumps of new-grown cow parsley, a bad habit I'd allowed him to indulge in over the years.

At the end of July, I watched Lucinda jump Gossip over some show-jumps. He bucketed into the fences pulling hard, acting like a five-year-old. But his wretched joint, after lying dormant all spring, started to complain. Veterinary expertise indicated that it might be as long as a year before Gossip would be able to partake in more strenuous exercise.

For Gossip to sit in the field for a year would be to consign him to purgatory, and at the end he would be a grouchy eighteen-year old, no longer able to seriously partake in the sport he loved so much.

Which is why, ten days later, Gossip galloped free, to do what he wanted, when he wanted, where no human could reach out to curb his spirit.

15 Epitaph
by Lucinda Green

When I think, as so often I do, of Village Gossip the word 'indomitable' immediately comes before my eyes followed by an impression of a dark-brown silky body seering at speed across my private viewing screen. A second later, I see this same figure repeatedly rearing in the back drive of Appleshaw, refusing to go down it any further. Such a horse I am unlikely ever to meet again in my life.

It took me two whole years to learn enough about him to begin to understand how to ride him across country and show-jumping. It took a further four years to begin to understand how he liked to be ridden in the dressage.

He was responsible for teaching me probably the most important lesson of my life, and one which is often never learnt: the ability to leave a horse alone.

Gossip would not tolerate domination of any sort; so sensitive, so single-minded was he, that he could not even bear being advised as to what pace he should approach a fence.

All that Be Fair and Wideawake had ever taught me about riding across country, about the need to steady and collect up before an awkward coffin, or sunken-road-type fence, I attempted to put into practice with Gossip. To no avail as it was virtually impossible to steady him, for he paid little enough attention to the bit. We tried so many different ones – everything, barring a plain metal eggbutt, rendering him unridable.

He was a very careful jumper and although he never fell or came near to it in those early days, our rounds both across country and show-jumping were not happy ones. There was little understanding between us and no harmony. We would turn in clear cross-country rounds but they were battles from before the start to the finish.

Then at Crookham, the first event of 1978, Gossip actually refused at a rail into a gulley and ran out at the next fence, a parallel. Anyone who rides has probably endured at some point that feeling of hopeless inadequacy. It enveloped me again, trying to ride Gossip, as it had done when trying to learn how to ride Wideawake.

Here was a brilliant little horse who, with Katie O'Hara, had twice shot round Tidworth three-day event and once around Burghley, producing breathtaking clear rounds each time, and I had eventually succeeded in making him refuse.

He was due to run at Badminton five weeks after that Crookham. There was no other horse that could run there, and OCL had just launched themselves into the sport with the first-ever major company sponsorship of a rider – me.

By the time Rushall arrived two weeks after Crookham, my dejection and desperation had combined to produce a conclusion: if, as I tried to control him, Gossip fought me so much that eventually his fighting overcame even his innate desire to jump, then I would not fight him. I would let him go at his own break-neck speed and sit it out, totally unconvinced of the wisdom of this resolve. But it had to be tried; there seemed no other alternative.

That round at Rushall, in very wet conditions across those solidly constructed fences is the one I remember the best with Gossip.

Without the added distraction of having to fight off my controlling efforts, Gossip took command. He galloped full tilt into everything and, just a few strides short of each fence he turned himself into a juddering pneumatic road-drill as he altered his own balance and power, and shortened and steadied his own stride in readiness to jump.

It was in this manner that he returned the incredibly fast times he did throughout his career. It was only as he aged considerably that he became increasingly more normal to ride and in consequence did not return quite such outrageous times.

Gossip's extraordinary ability was derived from more than

just his remarkable athleticism. He was not a horse of great scope; he needed speed to produce his jumping power, both show-jumping and across country. Where I think he found his three greatest allies were in his exceptional balance, his speed-of-light wit and his invincible courage. These last two worked against me in the dressage for many years until eventually I learnt to work with them.

I look back on the hot summer days that he and I spent in the school. I was at my wits' end trying to force Gossip to accept the bit. I tried everything I knew and searched for help from many; eventually, so many years later, I gave up on his dressage. I admitted defeat and therefore relaxed. I sat there and did nothing, and gradually, little by little, he too began to relax his highly tensed body and to both our amazement, he discovered the bit.

By this time he was already thirteen. I often wonder how different things could have been for him if I had admitted defeat considerably earlier.

I think probably most of us wonder how things would have been if we knew then what we know now. That, surely, is the eternal fascination of life, particularly where horses are concerned. It is one long, wide road of learning.

A teacher of the calibre of Village Gossip was a rare luxury.

Our relationship over the years had been so strong that I never noticed myself slowly falling in love with Gossip. I had always held him in tremendous respect and after the initial two years found his wickedness and his particular sense of humour very funny.

Genuine mutual affection was only apparent in the last few years, and because of the length of time it had taken to establish itself its roots were very deep.

The decision to send Gossip to Heaven was something I always hoped would never have to be taken, although I knew that he would never be happy living any life other than a fully active one that ably challenged his undiminishing aggression.

But, in tune with the beginning of our life together, the end was to be no easier.

Gossip was exceedingly well and he had returned from a few

days' team training with Regal Realm, where he had enjoyed a dazzling flat-out cross-country practice up on the Wylye downs.

But he had gone lame again on the joint that had been troubling him for some while.

The time to make the decision had finally presented itself. There was nothing to be gained by delay.

His departure left a vacuum in the hearts of those closest to him; a corner therein that will remain forever empty.

That particular brand of fire will never burn again.

Index